From Thinking to Li

THE WORK OF RUDOLF STE..

From the time that he was a medical student onwards, the driving force in Francis Edmunds' life was his quest for insight into the nature of the human being. This is what brought him to anthroposophy, led him into becoming a teacher and resulted in his wide travelling both to lecture and to encourage the development of new ventures born out of anthroposophy. In 1962 he founded Emerson College, an adult school for training and research based on Rudolf Steiner's work. Its students are now widely distributed throughout the world, themselves promoting new undertakings in education, agriculture and other related fields. This book is a new and revised edition of *Anthroposophy*, first published in 1982.

Rudolf Steiner

From Thinking to Living

THE WORK OF RUDOLF STEINER

Francis Edmunds

ELEMENT BOOKS

To my friends and students
in their several lands.

First published in 1982 as *Anthroposophy* by Carnant Books

This edition first published in 1990 by
Element Books Limited
Longmead, Shaftesbury, Dorset

Printed and bound by
Billings Ltd., Hylton Road, Worcester
Design by Humphrey Stone
Cover design by Max Fairbrother
Cover illustration Verlag am Goetheanum

British Library Cataloguing in Publication Data
Edmunds, Francis
[Anthroposophy] From thinking to living
1. Austrian philosophy. Steiner, Rudolf, 1861–1925
I. [Anthroposophy] II. Title
299′.935′0924

ISBN 1-85230-130-9

Contents

Introduction

IT IS NOT easy to find a compact but comprehensive introduction to the life and work of Rudolf Steiner. Many of his
works are still untranslated or are out of print. And while
there is now an extensive secondary literature in German,
there is rather little in English.

This may be partly because those who have encountered
Steiner's work in the English speaking world have been
fired to undertake all kinds of activities which have left them
little time to write. In recent years, Waldorf schools, (which
derive from the new school pioneered with Steiner's help in
Stuttgart in 1919), have been founded all over the world, as
have new homes and communities for handicapped children and adults. The new work in medicine, agriculture,
architecture, the arts, and even banking, which has developed strongly in continental Europe, is also beginning to be
better known in England, the United States and many other
parts of the world. The prophetic quality of Steiner's
thought, and the creative potential in the path he called
Anthroposophy, become ever more clearly apparent in our
times.

So a work of this kind, which is both a survey of Steiner's
extraordinary achievement and a personal testimony, is of
great value. It comes from a man whose life had been fired
and guided by Steiner's work, and who has played a major
part in bringing his impulses for education to life in the
Western world.

From his youth, Francis Edmunds lived as an idealist.
As a medical student, a relief worker in Russia, then as

a teacher, he saw with passion and compassion that the ills of the world are rooted in a crippled understanding of human nature. The scientific age tries to persuade us that we are fundamentally machines or animals, and so it is blind to the possibility that we may also be angels-in-the-making. Life shapes itself accordingly.

Impelled by a sense for human life as a journey of the spirit to discover and realize its true nature, on encountering Steiner's work he could see instantly that it contained both the vision and the path for which he had been searching. After the first world war he began teaching first at Friends' School in Lebanon for three years, and then at the International School in Geneva for two years before joining the first English Waldorf School in Streatham, London, in 1932.

He and a group of gifted colleagues carried this school through the second world war, to its present home in Forest Row, Sussex. In the 1950s, he began to visit the United States and help the developing Waldorf school movement there, inspiring parents, teachers and children alike. This activity he then extended to South Africa, Australia, New Zealand and Brazil.

During the second world war, he was increasingly preoccupied with questions of adult education. The impulse being realised in the Waldorf schools needed its continuation into further and higher education. The universities and colleges of the Western world are often citadels of that crippled view of nature and human nature which obscures the living creative spirit in both. How might there be founded adult centres for education and training which, as he later put it, spring from "a concept of the human being which can imbue life with grace and purpose and meaning"?

While in the United States, Francis Edmunds had come to recognise in the works of Ralph Waldo Emerson a nineteenth century spirit striving towards the ideals that Steiner began to realise in the twentieth. Accordingly, when in 1962, with the help of a group of English and American friends, he came to found a new centre for adult education, he chose for it the name Emerson College. In the years following, he devoted his main energies to building up the College, which began in connection with the Sunfield Childrens' Homes at Clent, and then moved to Forest Row in order to collaborate with Michael Hall school in teacher training. The College has now added to its original 'foundation year', further training in agriculture and the arts, as well as teaching, and draws students from all over the world.

Meanwhile, Francis Edmunds continued to travel widely, lecturing, teaching, supporting and encouraging new pioneering ventures born out of anthroposophy. Thus what he brings in this book has been not only thought but lived. For the true idealist, ideals are not simply attractive thoughts to be contemplated at one remove from reality, but are truths to be sought, found and realised in life itself. So this guide to Steiner's work has been engendered, as Steiner himself would certainly have wished it, not out of theory but out of a life lived to the full.

JOHN DAVY

Preface

It was shortly after World War 1 that, as a young medical student, I sat contemplating a human brain. The question that occupied me was what is it that thinks; can it be matter that thinks? What relation is there between this mass of matter and my immediate experience of thinking? What is thinking?

I looked outside. There I saw young men, a year or so older than myself, back from the trenches, some of them shattered in body and maybe also in mind. Why? What determined this? What ruled in life? That was my second question.

Descartes had said: "I think, therefore I am". Steiner reversed this into "I am, therefore I think". Either way, what am I? The third and most crucial question.

These are questions that everyone puts to himself who thinks at all. Can they be answered or are they unanswerable? This book, based on the teachings of Rudolf Steiner (1861–1925), sets out to offer at least an approach to answers.

Steiner grew up and reached his adult maturity during the last four decades of the nineteenth century, a period of time when materialism as an outlook was growing to a peak as the following remarkable sequence of developments must show: Darwinism; Marxism; the psychology of the subconscious; the mechanical theory of heat; the wave or corpuscular theory of light; the spectroscope offering confirmation of Newton's view of universal gravitation; electric power added to steam power; electro-magnetism, the electro-magnetic field, the discovery of the electron and radioactive substances; all this and much more in the space of less than forty years, leading on directly to the nuclear physics of the early twentieth century, the atomic bomb, the harnessing of nuclear energy so that the concept of matter itself has been disbanded. Along with all this we need to recall the immense progress in technology, and consequently in industry, and commerce, communication, and transport. For the ruling classes this added up to a time of growing prosperity and optimism for the future.

For the large working masses of the people things were different. Materially the great majority lived in poverty, largely illiterate and ignorant, an easy prey for the Marxist doctrine that possession was the road to freedom. The traditional faiths that had sustained life and hope for many were fast fading out. It was the job and the wages it offered that was the sustaining hope now, and there one was made subject to the boss.

Beneath the glitter of success there was gathering unease, discontent, and a growing sense of resentment, that must sooner or later lead of itself to change or to open conflict. Here were premonitions of hard and harder times to come.

Rudolph Steiner, standing at the turn of the century, with his higher faculties of vision, saw clearly the portents of pending disasters. It was a destiny moment of great import for the whole of humanity. There had to be an immense new step away from the illusive promises of materialistic thought towards the spirit; away from beholding man as the offspring of animal, or as a creature born of dust. There had to be a new evaluating of man's heroic achievements, through toil and struggle, out of his past, and a new beholding of his great potentials for the future. The spirit of man, now sunk in matter, has to awaken to the light of a new morning, the beginning of a long process through pain and struggle, for man to come to his spiritual birth. A turning point is but one point around which all else revolves. There were those who felt dimly that the nineteenth century marked the end of an epoch, but who could foresee what the character of the new epoch was to be? Who could have foreseen in the world catastrophes and widespread sufferings of the twentieth century, that these were the beginning labour pains of a new era, still far distant, but beginning now? If humanity is to survive, there must be this turning point which each must recognise in terms of himself, and which some will see as the promise of the Second Coming.

This is to be achieved not by a flight to mysticism or old world glories, but by patient and diligent labour for the cultivation of higher faculties of cognition. The disciplines acquired in arriving at a science of matter should not be lost but should be carried further by more advanced disciplines towards a science of the spirit. Rudolf Steiner, out of his own higher researches, states that there has always been a spiritual science since human life began. This has gone through many changes with the advancing conditions and needs of mankind from age to age. Whereas in the past such teachings were reserved for the chosen few (hence the word occult), to be disseminated by them through myth and legend to the many, it is his view that humanity has reached a stage, in this scientific age based on independent thought, when such teachings should be made available to all who are seriously enquiring for them. It is in this sense that this introductory book has been written.

April 1989

FRANCIS EDMUNDS
Founder of *Emerson College,*
(An adult school of study and research based on
Rudolf Steiner's work).
Forest Row,
East Sussex,
England.

The Way of Rudolf Steiner

(based on *The Course of My Life*)

GREAT SPIRITUAL teachers there have been throughout the ages. There could be no discord among them for they drew their wisdom from a single source. Yet each had to frame his teaching according to the needs of his time and this is true also of Rudolf Steiner. He was born into an age of acute scepticism in regard to spiritual matters. Materialistic thinking dominated, as it still does in the schools, and determines the practical conduct of life. We are fortunate to have his autobiography, *The Course of my Life* (written at the request of others), to help us to understand better the kind of man he was and the trials he had to go through. This chapter relates particularly to his life and work in the nineteenth century to prepare for his teaching of anthroposophy in the twentieth.

The Early Years

As a quite young child, Steiner had to learn that he was understood when he spoke of certain things, but not when he spoke of others. He carried a world within him from which those around him were excluded. He could enter their world but they could not enter his. Even before the age of eight he had learnt to distinguish between 'a world seen' and 'a world not seen'. This imposed on him a silence and great loneliness.

In the eyes of others he was a healthy, normal child, helpful in the home and able at school. He was not a dreamer; on the contrary, he was very attentive to the people he met and to what was going on around him. There was always one or another adult who inclined warmly towards him, but there was nothing about him, even in his parents' eyes, to mark him out as being quite exceptional.

At about the age of ten an event occurred unperceived by others, but for him decisive. He saw on the bookshelf of the assistant master of the school he was then attending a book on geometry, and was allowed to borrow it. It was a new subject to him. He describes how he plunged into it with enthusiasm. For weeks on end his mind was filled with "the coincidence, the similarity of triangles, squares, polygons". He racked his brains over the question "where do parallel lines meet?". The theorem of Pythagoras fascinated him. Geometry came to him as a revelation.

That one can live within the mind in the shaping of forms perceived only within oneself, entirely without impression upon the external senses, became for me the deepest satisfaction. I found in this a solace for the unhappiness which my unanswered questions had caused me. To be able to lay hold upon something in the spirit alone brought me an inner joy. I am sure that I learned through geometry to know happiness for the first time.

Joy and happiness are strong terms. Perhaps there was a dawning sense, which could scarce have been formulated at the time, that there might after all be the possibility of communicating about a world 'not seen', and being understood. The above description was written in retrospect very late in Rudolf Steiner's life. He then adds: "I should have been forced to feel the physical world as a sort of spiritual darkness if it had not received light from that side," that is from that inner world in which he "loved to live". Was not his task already declared for him? Was not humanity without that light living in a state of spiritual darkness, threatened, as a consequence, with rapid decline? Pure thinking, that is thinking not bound to the senses but as exercised in geometry, provided him with a ground on which to proceed further. The 'joy' was one of relief and release.

In my relation to geometry I must perceive the first budding forth of a conception which later gradually evolved within me. This lived within me more or less unconsciously during my childhood, and about my twentieth year took a definite and fully conscious form. I said to myself: "The objects and occurrences which the senses perceive are in space. But, just as this space is outside man, so there exists within man a sort of soul-space which is the scene of action of spiritual beings and occurrences." I could not look upon thoughts as something like images which the human being forms of things; on the contrary, I saw in them revelations of a spiritual world on this field of action in the soul . . . for the reality of the spiritual world was to me as certain as that of the physical. I felt the need, however, for a sort of justification of this assumption. I wished to be able to say to myself that the experience of the spiritual world is just as little an illusion as is that of the physical world. With regard to geometry, I said to myself: "Here one is *permitted* to know something which the mind alone through its own power experiences." In this feeling I found the justification for speaking of the spiritual world that I experienced just as the physical.

In geometry we exercise sense-free thinking. The senses can stimulate our thinking but thinking itself is freeborn within us. Once this distinction is made, it follows that it should be possible to grasp in pure thought the facts of higher knowledge brought forward by someone endowed with spiritual perception. It is to this faculty of 'pure thinking' that anthroposophy addresses itself. A great part of Rudolf Steiner's labour was to translate his higher knowledge into ideas and images which the thinking mind can then grasp in all freedom and make its own.

Seeing plants does not make one a botanist, nor does having spiritual perceptions make one a spiritual investigator. Rudolf Steiner has aptly been described as *A Scientist of the Invisible*, the title of a book about him by Canon A. P. Shepherd. He was an arduous worker. His formal training was in mathematics and science but he himself extended this to philosophy and the classics, all the time relating his outer studies to his inner life and vice versa. It was his especial task to bridge the abyss in modern life between inner and outer.

I felt in duty bound at that time to seek for the truth through philosophy. I had to study mathematics and natural science. I was convinced that I should find no relation with them unless I could place their findings on a solid foundation of philosophy. But I beheld a spiritual world *as reality*. In perfectly clear vision the spiritual individuality of everyone was manifest to me. This had in the physical body and in action in the physical world merely its expression. It united itself with that which came as a physical germ from the parents. The dead human being I followed on his way into the spiritual world. After the death of a schoolmate I wrote about this phase of my spiritual life to one of my former teachers who had continued to be a close friend of mine after my High School days. He wrote back to me with unusual affection, but he did not deign to say one word about what I had written regarding the dead schoolmate. But this is what happened to me always at that time in the matter of my perceptions of the spiritual world . . . No one would pay any attention to it.

There was one exception to this in the guise of "a simple man of the people", a herb gatherer who sold his medicinal plants to the Vienna apothecaries. "When with him, it was possible to look deep into the mysteries of nature. He carried on his back the bundle of medicinal plants, but in his

4

heart he had the findings which he had won from the spirituality of nature in the gathering of the herbs." He appears in the character of Felix Balde in Rudolf Steiner's *Four Mystery Dramas*, written many years later.

Such people are still to be met, though usually in remote places. The author met such a man at the centre of a Shetland island. He had gone to see a Druid circle that was there. Close by was a long single-storied building called a blackhouse, divided one half for the family and the other for the creatures. It was there he lived. There was a natural nobility about him. His blue eyes had an inward look. In the course of conversation he said, "We old ones have our regular meetings in order to keep alive the old wisdom", and later, rather sadly; "Our children go to school and learn reading and writing, and laugh at what we know." In him and his ageing companions there were still 'souls which see'. They bore witness to a seeing which preceded the modern life of thought. The time has come for our thinking to grow to a new art of seeing. That is what anthroposophy is about.

The life of thought came gradually to seem to me the reflection radiated into the physical human being out of what the soul experiences in the spiritual world. Thought experience was for me existence in a reality – as something actually experienced through and through – doubt dared not approach. The world of the senses did not seem to me so completely a matter of experience. It is present but one does not lay hold upon it as upon thought. Yet man himself is set in the midst of this world. Then the question arose: Is *this* world, then, a reality complete in itself? When the human being weaves thoughts out of his inner being in connection with it which bring light into the world of the senses, is he actually bringing into this world something which is foreign to it? This certainly does not accord with the experience that we have when we confront the world of the senses and break into it by

5

means of our thoughts. Thought, then, surely appears to be that by means of which the world of the senses experiences *its own nature*. The further development of this reflection was at that time an important part of my inner life.

That we are able in some degree to enter into Rudolf Steiner's own struggles to attain the clarity he sought on such fundamental issues comes to us as a very special gift through his *Course of my Life*. For example, even whilst at High School, out of his bare earnings by coaching fellow students, he scraped together enough to purchase a copy of Kant's *Critique of Pure Reason*. Kant was then considered supreme amongst philosophers. He subscribed to the eighteenth century slogan "mathematics is the key to the Universe", a mathematics which underlay the mechanistic-materialistic view of the universe, whilst at the same time maintaining his belief in a moral world order. Thus the world was split into two irreconcilable halves, a view which was in direct contradiction to Rudolf Steiner's experience.

How relate to a world held in movement by the dead laws of inertia through endless space and time? At this point help came again from geometry and the new concepts arising from it.

A decisive experience came to me at that time precisely from the side of mathematics. The conception of space gave me the greatest inner difficulty. As the illimitable, all-encompassing void – the form in which it lay at the basis of the dominant theories of contemporary science – it could not be conceived in any definite manner. Through the more recent (synthetic) geometry which I learned through lectures and through private study, there came into my mind the perception that a line prolonged infinitely toward the right hand would return again from

6

the left to the starting point. The infinitely distant point on the right is the same as the infinitely distant point on the left. . . . The straight line returning on itself like a curve seemed to me to be a revelation. I left the lecture at which this had first passed through my mind as if a great load had fallen from me. A feeling of liberation came over me again, as in early boyhood, something joy-bestowing had come to me out of geometry.

Immediately following he writes:

Behind the riddle of space stood at that time in my life the riddle of time. Ought a conception to be possible there also which would contain within itself in idea a return out of the past into the 'infinitely distant' future. My happiness over the space concept caused me profound unrest over that of time. But there was then no visible way out. All effort of thought led me only to the realization that I must beware of applying the perceptible spacial concept to that of time. All the disappointments which can arise from the striving for knowledge were experienced in connection with the riddle of time.

If we take as the meaning of infinite that which is not finite and cannot be confined to any given measure, (as for instance in infinite Father, infinite love, compassion, devotion and so on), then in breaking away from the idea of mere endlessness of space and time we come a little closer to the heart of the question.

In point of fact, this problem of time led to a totally new conception of repeated earth lives: past experience transmuted in the course of its passage through the spiritual worlds through the 'infinite' morality of divine being, returns newly gifted and circumstanced for shaping a new life. Past is transmuted into future. Along these lines the idea of re-incarnation enters the domain of a science scarcely

7

begun as yet, the science of metamorphosis of which Goethe was a great pioneer.

We wish in these pages to show that anthroposophy is not something simply to be received but to be striven for. It is in promoting such inner striving that its mission lies, for in that way alone can genuine progress arise. And always it calls for clear thinking and discriminating judgement. The twentieth century has raised many questions about the nature of science and the way it is going. James Jeans in his *Physics and Philosophy* states quite baldly that much that was assumed to be objective turns out to consist of 'subjective mental constructs'. Certain values have been selected in deliberate disregard of others and theories built up on them. Arthur Eddington, like Jeans a prominent astro-physicist, in *The Nature of the Physical World* compares the physicist's construction of the universe to a house that Jack built leaving in it no room for Jack. W. J. N. Sullivan, in his book *Limitation of Science*, writes the following:

> We see that the scientific outlook, as presented by Galileo, constitutes a really amazing revolution in thought. The vivid world of the mediaevalist, a world shot through with beauty, and instinct with purpose, a world having an intimate relationship to his own destiny, and an intelligible reason for existing in the light of that destiny, is dismissed as an illusion. It has no objective existence. The real world, as revealed by science, is a world of material particles, moving in accordance with mathematical laws, through space and time.

Rudolf Steiner as a student entered deeply into the scientific theories holding sway. He was specially concerned at one time with the mechanical theory of heat and the wave theory of light.

At that time the external physical world was conceived as

motion-processes in matter. Sensations seemed to be only subjective processes, the effects of pure motion upon the senses of the human being. Out there in space, it was assumed, occur motion-processes in matter; if these processes affect the human sense for heat, the sensation of heat is experienced. Outside of man are wave-processes in ether; if these affect the optic nerve, light and colour sensations are generated. This conception met me everywhere. It caused me unspeakable difficulties in my thinking. It banished all spirit from the objective external world.

What position in view of this was he to adopt? He goes on:

Even so I could not yet resolve to oppose a manner of thinking of my own, even for myself alone, against that which then prevailed. But just this caused me bitter soul struggles. Again and again the criticism I could easily formulate against this way of thinking had to be suppressed within me to await a time when more comprehensive sources and ways of knowledge could give me greater assurance.

Out of his wrestling with such questions came Rudolf Steiner's doctoral thesis, *Truth and Science*, and later, his *Philosophy of Freedom*. Later still came his lecture courses on heat, on light, also on astronomy, opening up quite new ways of research. He had the highest regard for all that the scientists were able to discover, but they stopped dead at the frontiers to the spirit. They had acquired an immense knowledge of outer data without entry into what lived within. This is equally true of the biological sciences. What rules in the multitudinous forms in nature, what quickens the life in plants, what wakens the sense life in the animals, what mounts as thinking spirit in man? It is to these sciences that Rudolf Steiner now turns.

9

I observed the members of the human, animal and plant organism in their formations – I became more and more aware that the picture of nature which is attainable through the senses penetrates through to that which was visible to me in a spiritual way.

If in this spiritual way I directed my look to the soul activity of the human being, in thinking, feeling and willing, the 'spiritual man' took form for me even as a clearly visible image. I could not linger in the abstractions of which it is customary to think when speaking of thinking, feeling and willing. In these inner manifestations of life I saw creative forces which placed the 'human being as spirit' spiritually before me. If I then directed my look to the sense appearance of man, this was supplemented to my reflective contemplation through the spirit-form which holds sway in the sense-perception.

Concerning his further researches into this subject he wrote, "My look fell, at first in a very imperfect way, upon the threefold organization of the human being, about which – after having pursued my study of it for thirty years in silence – I first began to speak publicly in my book *Riddles of the Soul*."

This gives us a glimpse into what such work entailed, what patient labour spread over decades, before the results were ready to be shared with others. The threefold knowledge of man becomes a master key to the understanding not only of man but of the whole world related to him.

Steiner and Goethe

A powerful factor in Rudolf Steiner's life was the work he did on Goethe, both the poet and the scientist. As a poet Goethe is universally acknowledged, as scientist hardly at all even to this day, though he himself believed his science would outlive his poetry.

As to Goethe the poet, the author had the opportunity of

finding himself in the company of outstanding Goetheanists in Britain. They could not eulogize sufficiently about him as a poet and sage, but there was only one who concerned himself seriously with his science. *Faust*, part two, they found largely incomprehensible, attributing this to the fact that Goethe wrote it in his old age. It may be mentioned that the immense work of *Faust* part one and two is performed at regular two-yearly intervals unexpurgated and with great artistry at the Goetheanum in Dornach near Basle, the world centre of the Anthroposophical Society. Rudolf Steiner gave many lectures on Faust and other of Goethe's literary works. We might also mention how he felt at one time a need to meditate on the fairy tale *The Green Snake and the Beautiful Lily* and how after twenty-one years it appeared transformed in his first mystery play, *The Portal of Initiation*.

It is for his work on Goethe the scientist that the world owes much to him, though this too has so far been little acknowledged. Some of his followers, activated by him, have continued research along Goetheanistic lines, but to the world at large Goethe's outlook on nature remains unfamiliar or at best, enigmatic.

It was while Rudolf Steiner the student was preoccupied with questions of light and colour, not satisfied with the current explanations based on Newton, that he first came across Goethe's work.

We will not enter here into the controversy that has raged around the Goethean theory of colour as opposed to that of Newton. If rage is the word, then Goethe raged against Newton, and the rest of the world, with rare exceptions, raged against Goethe. We need however, to mention briefly the contrasting circumstances, for they reflect back on the men.

Newton placed a prism in the path of a beam of white light and saw a band of colours appear on a screen. Placing another prism in reverse he saw the colours vanish again into a white beam. He concluded that the colours were already contained within the white light. On emergence they were dispersed according to their different refractive indices and then were re-assembled as white light. Being the mathematician he was, he arrived at a mathematical scale to match the colours and this has served industry well, for the scale can be used to determine any shade of colour within the spectrum.

With Goethe the matter took a different course. He clapped the prism to his eye expecting to see the spectrum of which he had read. Instead he saw two bands of colour, a light and a dark one and no green between them at all. Only when the two bands were drawn together to overlap, did the green appear as a secondary effect. Goethe was greatly interested in the *qualities* of colours, and for him the primary phenomenon lay in the contrasting two bands. These he interpreted as the interplay of the forces of light and darkness. He saw darkness as an active power in the world in opposition to light. Where darkness intervenes between the eye and the object, as with a sinking sun, the brightness of the sun is dimmed down to red. On the other hand where light streams in between the eye and the object, as in gazing at distant hills or at the sky, darkness is raised to blue. Goethe went so far as to describe colours as the deeds and sufferings of light – something which to others is unwarranted fantasy.

But then, Goethe saw the whole of life in terms of polarity. He saw the root of the plant contracting into the earth, and the blossoms unfolding towards the wideness of the heavens, and the leaf mediating variously between the below and the above. For Goethe light and darkness, joy and grief, elation and depression, were equally polaric realities within the life of soul. So were night and day, winter and summer polarities, also outer life and the life within, each had its counterpart in the other. Life and death also expressed such a polarity, as the following lines by

Goethe, often quoted by Rudolf Steiner show:

> And as long as thou knowest it not,
> This dying and becoming,
> Thou art but a troubled guest
> Upon the dark earth.

The whole wondrous world of colours with all their expressiveness was dead, laid out in the spectrum. It left one blind to their living qualities. It was like robbing life of meaning. It was this that troubled Goethe so deeply.

How then did Rudolf Steiner enter into all this? Being fully familiar with the usual experimentation with light and colour and also with the mathematical treatment of optics, he could say:

> In spite of all objections raised by the physicist against Goethe's theory of colour, I was driven by my own experiments further away from the customary view and toward Goethe. I said to myself that colours are not, as Newton thinks, produced out of light: they come to manifestation when obstructions hinder the free unfolding of light. But light was thus removed for me from the category of truly physical elements of reality. It presented itself as a midway stage between the realities perceptible to the senses and those visible to the spirit.
>
> I was not inclined to engage in merely philosophical processes of thinking about these things. But I laid strong emphasis upon *reading the facts of nature aright*. It then became constantly clearer to me that light itself does *not* enter the realm of the sense perception, but remains on the farther side of this, while colours appear when the sense perceptible is brought into the realm of light.

We see Newton standing in a dark room, aware of the light streaming in, but ignoring the darkness, and thus concluding that the colours are produced out of the light and must therefore be already contained in the light.

We see Goethe with his whole disposition, taking his place as artist between the light and the darkness, and perceiving the colours arising through a struggle between them.

We imagine Steiner standing consciously within the light which is itself invisible to the senses, gazing out into nature which would be all in darkness without that light, and beholding the colours arising where sensible nature reaches into the supersensible light.

Newton as observer stands within the sensible world. That is all he is concerned with and he translates the phenomena accordingly.

Goethe the artist experiences life and nature as a process of interplay between the sensible and the supersensible. He even coined the expression: *sinnlich-sittlich*, to behold the world both with the outer senses and with inner perception of the *idea* creative in the phenomenon.

Steiner stands at home in the supersensible world, and beholds the physical world in its spiritual aspect. Thus in pursuing his study of living organisms he could write: "I came upon the *sensible-supersensible* form of which Goethe speaks, which is interposed, both for true natural vision and also for spiritual vision, between what the senses grasp and what the spirit perceives."

This that interposes itself he described later as a realm of etheric formative forces, that shapes all forms to outer visibility. Goethe had trained himself to perceive this hidden creative ideal element at work in nature, so that he could claim actually *to see ideas* with the same clarity as others who see only the outer object. It is thus he could speak of the *archetypal plant* which manifested throughout the plant kingdom in varying degrees from the simplest to the highest forms. For Goethe the archetypal plant became a major discovery following many years of close study of the plant kingdom. It was there for his inner eye as a potent reality. To others, even to Schiller, it appeared to be only an abstract idea.

For Rudolf Steiner it was Goethe himself who was the major discovery of his student days. And then, on the recommendation of his teacher, Karl Julius Schröer, a noted Goetheanist, it came about that in 1884, in his twenty-third year, he was invited to edit Goethe's scientific writings "with introductions and running explanatory comments", for what was to be a standard publication, Kürschner's *German National Literature* series. In order to try and make Goethe's work more understandable to others he wrote *The Theory of Knowledge Implicit in Goethe's World Conception*, published in 1886.

In 1895, he wrote a further volume, *Goethe's World Conception*. The work he undertook stretched to five volumes and was not completed till 1897. He was also invited to edit some hitherto unpublished work of Goethe lying in the archives at Weimar. He thus spent years living in Weimar with others likewise engaged on work on Goethe. That Goethe has been acknowledged as a pioneer of a new science of morphology is in large measure due to Steiner's work.

He writes: "Long before Kepler and Copernicus, men saw the processes in the starry heavens. These two first discovered the laws of these occurrences. Long before Goethe, organic nature was investigated. Goethe discovered its laws. Goethe is the Copernicus and Kepler of the organic world." Elsewhere he speaks of him similarly as the Galileo of organic nature.

Steiner also wrote a book, *Goethe as the Founder of a New Science of Aesthetics*, in which artist and scientist meet in their different yet complementary roles, a view that is close to the heart of anthroposophy.

In his work on Goethe the endeavour was to enter deeply into Goethe's nature and to see and interpret the world through his eyes. Rudolf Steiner acknowledges that to carry this through, whilst continuing with his own research, was a great discipline toward developing even greater objectivity with regard to his own work.

During these years there was shaping in his mind *The Philosophy of Freedom* which was to provide a sure foundation for the anthroposophy to come.

The Nature of Thinking
(with reference to The Philosophy of Freedom*)*

As the years went by, Rudolf Steiner came into intimate contact with many interesting people wrestling in their different ways with the problems of life. Try as he would he could find no way of communicating to them what to him was most vital. He remained isolated in himself. His endeavours to elucidate what Goethe had been striving for brought only a dubious response.

> I had a conversation with a physicist who was an important person in his field and also who occupied himself intensively with Goethe's conception of nature. The conversation came to a climax in his saying that Goethe's conception with respect to colours was such that physics could not do anything whatever with it – and in my *becoming silent*.
>
> How much there was then which indicated that what was truth to me was of such a character that the thought of the time "could do nothing whatever with it".

And so it was in all things. He was the conscious bearer of an inner world of reality of which humanity had dire need, but he could find no entry to the minds of even his closest friends. They could only conclude that, capable as he was and practical, he was nevertheless caught up in some kind of dream.

He writes:

> I entered with vital intensity into what others perceived

and thought, but I could not make my own inner spirituality to flow into this world I thus experienced. As to my own being, I had always to remain behind within myself. Indeed, my world was separated as if by a thin partition from all the outer world . . . .
Thus it was with persons, and also with world views. I liked to be with Suphan; I liked to be with Hartleben. Suphan never called on Hartleben; Hartleben never called on Suphan. Neither could enter into the characteristic ways of thinking and feeling of the other. With Suphan and equally with Hartleben I was immediately as at home. But neither Suphan nor Hartleben ever came to me. Even when they came to me, they really remained with themselves. In my spiritual world I could experience no visit.

The question ever remained: "How can a way be found whereby that which is inwardly beheld as true may be set forth in such forms of expression as can be understood by this age?"
What is this age? It is an age when man set out to explore the world anew, independent of the past; an age of knowledge to be built on the evidence of the physical senses alone; an age of Natural Science to the exclusion of all consideration of anything transcending the purely physical; an age therefore of scepticism and agnosticism in which only materialistic thinking prevailed. Man, in the light of this thinking, is no more than a complex piece of matter subject to physical and chemical analysis like any other piece of matter, all his attributes being regarded as effects of matter; an age in which man appears to have lost sight of himself.
The consequence is that the expectations of growing freedom through emancipation from past restraints has resulted in conditions of rapidly increasing unfreedom. This was becoming apparent in the nineteenth century and has become sharply evident since. Knowledge in its present

form has divorced life on earth from purposeful meaning. How could one endowed with spiritual perception speak to men in our time? This was the formidable question that lay upon Rudolf Steiner and that he had to solve.

Many, on first coming to anthroposophy, wonder why such emphasis is placed on thinking. Rudolf Steiner tells that he might have set out what he had to give in mythological form. Appealing thus through pictures and images directly to the feelings, progress might have been rapid. We live, however, in an age where the intellectual faculty is paramount, an age which prides itself on building up its knowledge on the basis of independent observation and thought. This was therefore the rock on which he had to build.

The form of expression in the realm of the natural sciences consists in content-filled ideas, even though the content might be materialistically conceived. I desired to form ideas that bear upon the spiritual world in the same way as natural-scientific ideas bear upon the physical.

But then, how is one to regard thinking itself? Are thoughts merely the result of the impress of sense-impressions upon the mind, or are they engendered from within man to take hold of the life of the senses? In regard to this question Rudolf Steiner writes explicitly:

In sense-perception man faces the world as illusion. But when, from within man himself, sense-free thinking follows after sense-perception, illusion is then permeated with reality; it ceases to be illusion. The human spirit experiencing itself within, then meets the Spirit of the World, now no longer concealed from man behind the sense-world, but living and moving within the sense-world.

How then is one to regard materialism?

> I perceived the harmful character of this way of thinking
> not in the fact that the materialist directs his attention to
> the material form of manifestation of a being, but in the
> way he conceives the material. He contemplates *matter*
> without becoming aware that he is really in the presence
> of *spirit* which is simply manifesting itself in the form of
> matter.... Spirit must first take on the form of a material
> brain in order to lead in this form the life of the conceptual
> world, which can bestow upon man in his earthly life
> freely acting self-consciousness. To be sure, in the brain
> spirit mounts upward out of matter, but only after the
> material brain has arisen out of spirit.

Rudolf Steiner is at pains to show in his later work how in
the course of the ages the human spirit descended more and
more deeply into matter, we will return to this later. This
led, on the one hand, to a diminishing awareness of the
spiritual world and, over against this, to an accentuated
awareness of self. In the present age of science this dual
process has reached a climax. Man finds himself completely
cut off from the spiritual world but strongly centred in his
isolated sense of selfhood.

He is so far cut off that he cannot even truly find his
fellow human beings. Yet in this very fact lives the secret
of the age, man's growing need to cross the boundaries
that separate him from others and from the world. What
might appear at the surface as the greatest loss could
be the opportunity for the greatest gain. If the separation
is to be surmounted by conscious effort and in freedom,
it can only be, to begin with, on the ground of pure,
sense-free, self-reliant thinking. This carried forward could
lead the science of nature to a science of the spirit, from
the world of the 'seen' to the world of the 'not seen',
so that man may, once again, feel himself united with
higher reality.

Rudolf Steiner, at the age of twenty-seven or twenty-eight, whilst deeply engaged in his work on Goethe, was at the same time profoundly concerned with establishing a bridge from natural science, despite its present materialistic character, to the worlds of the spirit which were, we might say, waiting at man's call. He could describe the situation as he then saw it in the following way:

Whoever recognizes as an attribute of thinking its capacity of perception extending beyond the apprehension through the senses must necessarily also attribute to thinking objects existing beyond the limits of mere sense-perceptible realities. But these objects of thinking are Ideas.

As thinking takes possession of the Idea, it merges with the primordial foundation of the world; that which works without enters into the spirit of man; he becomes one with objective reality at its highest potency.

In other words, man is no longer confined to an outer seeing of the world but begins to perceive, to begin with in ideas, the shaping powers at work within the phenomena. (We recall Goethe's perception of the archetypal plant.)

Rudolf Steiner:

I wished to express the truth that nature is in reality spiritual. I wished to show that man, *in thinking*, does not form conceptions regarding nature while standing outside her, but that knowing means *experiencing*, so that, while knowing, man is inside the being of things.

Further:

Being aware of the Idea within reality is communion of man.

Each has to reach and take hold of the Idea himself, yet it is just in this realm that men can truly find one another in total freedom and in perfect fellowship. This is to find one another in the spirit, the first, essential step towards rediscovering the worlds of the spirit.

"Thinking," wrote Rudolf Steiner, "has the same significance in relation to Ideas as the eye has for light, the ear for sound: it is the organ of perception."

All this is so remote from the common view of things that it may call for great initial effort to make it real to oneself, but it then comes as an amazing discovery. It means no less than that in coming to a new realization of the character of one's own thinking, we also come to a new relationship with our very selves, with our fellow human beings and with the whole world order. We begin to confront life from a totally new vantage point. We are no longer wanderers astray in a strange and remote world but have a secure ground under us from which to re-examine and re-evaluate all previous values and experiences. It is thus far that Rudolf Steiner can bring us in his *Philosophy of Freedom*, published in 1894 when he was thirty-three.

But the book was not understood. The moment it was off the press he sent a copy to the one person he thought might understand, an older man to whom he looked with reverence as an enlightened thinker. He waited expectantly and full of hope. The volume came back, most painstakingly annotated with comments and observations but showing that what the book really stood for had been totally misunderstood.

However, as with the work on Goethe, so with the work on *The Philosophy of Freedom*, it had been faithfully carried through. In the alchemy of life, and in the course of years, understanding began to grow until there are many who would say it marked a turning point in their approach to life. The book is there to be read. Whilst it is not intended greatly to enlarge on it here, there are some comments concerning the book which the author thinks may be helpful.

First, there is a question. *The Philosophy of Freedom* first appeared in 1894 – a long time ago. Up to the present it is only most rarely referred to in any formal course on philosophy. Why is that?

The answer, of course, lies in the nature of the book. It is not a philosophy as ordinarily understood, that is, as the expression of a particular thinker setting out his views on life. There are many philosophers and each one presents his personal outlook. *The Philosophy of Freedom* cannot be described in that way. It is not a Steiner philosophy, but rather a study into the nature of thinking.

The basic principle is that thinking as an activity arises within the human being in the form of ideas or concepts. Thinking has to be about something and that something stands before one as an object perceived, a percept. When the concept and the percept relate rightly, there where they meet and there alone do we in our experience touch reality. Only the human being can bring about this meeting of concept and percept – only each one for himself – in this lies the road to freedom.

This book shows three levels at which this meeting takes place.

The first relates to the life of the senses. The senses bring to us an object or percept. To take hold of that percept in an act of cognition, we have to give birth to the answering concept. However, since every percept that comes towards us by way of the physical senses is born of the past, it follows that our conceptual life, our concepts, are likewise related to the past. This characterizes our present-day scientific outlook built as it is entirely on the 'supposed' view of the past.

The second level of meeting of concept with percept rests within the human being himself. He brings forward an idea – this idea he can contemplate in the same way as any other percept. If we would cognize that which is thus brought forward, though not of the senses, we have all the same to bring a concept towards it. It is thus that a system of mathematics arises, wholly in the mind, how Euclidean geometry was built up and more recently synthetic geometry – how a philosophy, or other construction wholly of the mind, is evolved. This is a process which rests entirely in the present. Here we are in the realm of cognitive experience, independent of the outer world of the senses, a thinking activity as a creative process which rests upon the faculty of engendering the percept we cognize through the concept and in the immediate present.

There is a third level at which concept and percept meet. It will be seen that every thought arises as an act of intuition – it is brought to light from within. There arise in this way what Rudolf Steiner calls moral intuitions, which lift to consciousness as moral imaginations such as truth, beauty, goodness. These, too, are ideas arising in the mind, we might also say in the spirit, as percepts to be observed and met by answering concepts. Here, however, the percept by its very nature transcends our present state of being. We may cognize truth, beauty, goodness but at the same time realize how far we fall short. They stand before us as a call from the 'as yet not', to the 'yet to be'. But in striving towards that future, we ourselves are changed from what we are to what we hope to become. At this level the cognitional act takes us ourselves into the future. Thus, in so far as thinking is related to sense experience we commune with the past; in evolving a structure of thought within ourselves we commune with the present; in the contemplation of ideas that stand before us as ideals we commune with the future.

Thinking, therefore has a threefold character related to past, present and future. To grasp this is to meet reality in all its aspects, but the achievement can only be by individual effort as an act of freedom – hence the title of the book, *The Philosophy of Freedom*. This is just one illustration of a far reaching exercise contained in the book. We begin to understand how with the idea, we live within creation, at one with the Creator.

Anthroposophy, a Way to Higher Knowledge

THE PUBLICATION of *The Philosophy of Freedom* still left unanswered the question of how Anthroposophy itself was to come into the world. To Rudolf Steiner it was clear "that the turn of the century must bring a new spiritual light to humanity", but how was this to come about?

In 1897 he left Weimar for Berlin. Soon after his arrival there he was offered the editorship of a long established cultural magazine. After three years, seeing he could not carry it further usefully he gave it up.

It was from this time on that Rudolf Steiner began to be increasingly in demand as a lecturer by various groups in search of new values. It was thus he came to give a lecture to a Giordano Bruno Union contrasting dualism with monism, then a second lecture of which he wrote, "It was my basic anthroposophical lecture and the starting point for my anthroposophical work".

Thus, too, he came to lecture to a theosophical gathering on "Goethe's hidden Revelation". Of this he wrote that in dealing with the fairy tale, "The Green Snake and the Beautiful Lily" he became "entirely esoteric . . . It was an important experience for me to be able to speak in words from the world of spirit after having been forced by circumstances throughout my Berlin period up to that time only to let the spirit shine through my presentation".

It was in this more restrained form that he gave whole lecture cycles on such fundamental themes as Christianity as Mystical Fact; Buddha to Christ; The Mystics of the Renaissance; Riddles of Philosophy; and others. Though born and ratified out of his spiritual research, they asked for no more than an open-minded attitude at a cultural level.

Increasingly he felt the need for a publication of his own, distinct from theosophical and other literatures, in which he could express himself as freely as he wished and reach out to a wider public. Thus, in the summer of 1903, there appeared the first issue of his monthly journal *Lucifer* (later called *Lucifer-Gnosis*). In this he gave out in sequel form the content of what later constituted his basic anthroposophical book, *Knowledge of Higher Worlds and how to Attain it.*

The name Lucifer for the journal occasioned questioning. Rudolf Steiner was using the word in its original meaning of Light-Bearer as, for instance, in the expression, "Christus versus Luciferus" "Children of Lucifer" meant, at that time, all who were striving for wisdom, for inner light. Goethe's Faust can be regarded, in this sense, as representative of modern striving man. We may remember that the journal *Lucifer* was launched at the turning point from Kali Yuga, the Age of Darkness, to the dawning of a new Age of Light.

This manner of openly communicating spiritual knowledge met with serious objections from some quarters. It was Rudolf Steiner's view, however, that the time had come when every human being had a right to whatever knowledge might be helpful to him. To this view he held always. The opening sentence reads: "There slumber in every human being faculties by means of which he can acquire for himself a knowledge of higher worlds."

For the years 1902–1912, Rudolf Steiner served as General Secretary of the German section of the Theosophical Society, though making it clear from the first that his teaching was based on his own spiritual research. Differences arose from time to time. These came to a head with the unwarranted announcement that a certain young Hindu was a reincarnation of Christ. The young man, to his lasting credit, repudiated this. He was none other than the late Krishnamurti who with his unswerving integrity, his practical wisdom and ever-ready helpfulness, gained the admiration and high esteem of thousands of adherents, from both East and West. For Steiner, that such a statement could be made at all, being so utterly out of accord with the truth, marked the end of his association with that Society. Those who held with him formed the core of what was to grow into the Anthroposophical Society. He now had his own audience with which he could work in untrammeled fashion. The question which had stood long before him, "must one be silent?" was now resolved.

His lectures Rudolf Steiner gave to variously assembled audiences. *Lucifer-Gnosis*, however, was addressed to all. He saw it as his task to share his spiritual knowledge as widely as possible. *The Philosophy of Freedom* had paved the way for this. In his journal he set out a carefully ordered series of exercises, intimate in style as from a teacher to his pupils, yet in every sense free. They are intended to lead by sure and certain stages along a path of inner development. The initiative, however, is left for each one to take according to his own independent judgement.

Types of Exercises

No more will be attempted here than to indicate in an elementary way the nature and scope of some of the early exercises and how they relate to one another.

For anyone embarking seriously on a path to higher knowledge there are certain prerequisites to be observed. They seem obvious yet need to be mentioned. First and foremost, Rudolf Steiner stresses the need to cultivate reverence for life and devotion to truth; then to strive always for clear thinking, balanced feeling, and a steadfast will; further, ever and again to recall the *golden rule*: For every step in knowledge, three steps in moral development. The goal of one's striving is service to life. It is well to recognize how far we have all been the victims, from birth on, of the negative effects of mass media and mechanization. The exercises, in addition to all else, are restorative of health; they would make us whole. We stand in certain relationships to life simply through our constitution as human beings: our relationship to the world around us through our physical senses; our relationship to time through the force of memory without which we should be utterly lost; then our dependence on others in the course of the years from birth in the shaping of our biography; finally, what we owe to ourselves in motivating our endeavours. The four exercises we are about to describe follow, in the main, the opening sections of *Knowledge of Higher Worlds*.

First then with regard to the life of the senses: By way of an example, we place a plant before us and observe it with all the care possible. We regard its form, colour, the succession of its parts, and so on. We then reflect on what we cannot see, the living entity that maintains and shapes the plant from stage to stage. The plant, as regards our senses, is part 'seen', part 'not seen', part revealed and part concealed. The part 'not seen' is waiting for us to develop another, a higher form of seeing. We repeat this exercise day after day, uniting our reflections with the accompanying feelings. This develops a gentle quality of alertness for all that meets us in life part revealed and part concealed. As with all such exercises, our responsibility rests on the faithfulness with which we carry them out. Having performed the exercise we set it aside and proceed with our normal day's work. We do not wait anticipating results but rest upon the doing. The fruits will show themselves in their own time.

The next exercise calls for a similar heightening of attentiveness, this time towards the field of memory. In the course of a day we pass through a host of impressions. It is as though life were beckoning to us at every turn. What we have consciously observed, we are able to recall as pictures in the mind.

This is quite a different seeing from that of the senses. We are gazing into a realm concealed from the outer senses. We are gazing into time. Let us select one of the many situations in which we find ourselves and re-create it as vividly as possible. But now we are warned against looking back merely introspectively, focussing our attention on ourselves in order to re-experience what we have already experienced. The intention of the exercise is, rather, that we should look away from ourselves to all that surrounded us at the time. Was it a sunset we were enjoying: it was the sunset that called out the joy in us. Was it a child in his innocent play that drew our attention, or a beggar by the wayside? Was it a stranger who came knocking on our door to ask the way? Was it a familiar or an unfamiliar voice on the telephone bringing good news, bad news? Was it the sight of the early snow-drops lifting their heads from the ground? What a host of eventfulness surrounds us all the time, playing towards us, with us, in us! Whatever it was that was outside us is now within us, it has entered into the stream of time, *our* time. Outside in space it might have been for all to see and experience. Now it has become an intrinsic part of ourselves, present for us alone. Memory gives us a ground to stand on, a ground of continuity within the otherwise vanishing passage of time. Time is no longer a juxtaposition of events occurring in space. The world of time reveals itself as an unfolding into space. We see it unfolding in the plant. We see it unfolding in the child, in ourselves also – a manifestation of growing and becoming and passing away. It is really time that carries space in its arms.

The physical body that I see with my eyes is perpetually changing, being cast off and being recreated, they say, every seven years. The physical substance is in a constant state of flow but the image remains, the form is retained. So, too, events pass by, but the memory remains. The form and the memory belong together. They are manifestations of what we may call a time-body, or in anthroposophy, an etheric or formative force body. It is the world out of which the visible world is shaped and we ourselves are membered in that world. To us is given the power to re-member ourselves in thought into situations that have gone by.

As the first exercise belongs to the world of the senses, the senses being part of our physical body, so we have a body in the realm of time. We are consciously living in a process of time and our awareness of ourselves is built on our memories. With the first exercise in regard to the plant we also became aware of a time-process but outside us. With the second exercise we are ourselves within the time-process.

The third exercise also relates to time but differently. We are concerned now with events and encounters which break in on the course of our lives, bringing major changes in the tenor, the direction, even the character of our lives. We meet a stranger who becomes a close associate, maybe even an intimate friend, a partner in life, perhaps through marriage or in some other connection. We live through an illness or maybe a serious accident which marks a turning point in our life. We experience the death of someone close to us and confront the mystery of death as never before; this may well lead to a deepening of our whole attitude to life. We pick up a book, as though by chance, and it may be the starting point of a new quest in life. We waken with an idea which opens up a new vista for us, and so on. What may not happen in the course of a lifetime? Are such events, which come like interventions, to be attributed only to chance? In retrospect they play a most significant part in shaping our lives and in determining our biography. We select one or another such experience in our life, something preferably that happened a time back so that we are not immediately emotionally involved. Again and again as we confront such a past experience, recalling the people who have entered our life at this or that point in our history, the impression may grow in us that there is indeed another world beyond those of space and time, a world to which we owe the drama of existence with its pains and joys, its meetings and partings, now comedy and now tragedy, laughter and tears, a world that pervades all life. To this world also belongs the Mystery of the Fall and the hope of redemption – and the dream that this old, old world will one day grow young again.

But now, to return to the exercise in question, to perform it truly requires the greatest possible degree of objectivity, of freedom from self. Here more than ever, one is warned not to fall into introspection, but to learn to regard oneself with the calmness of a judge confronting a stranger. This way of looking at things opens new possibilities. We may have suffered a death in the house. Our neighbour has suffered a similar loss. Ordinarily our grief at our own loss far outweighs the sorrow we share with our neighbour. Yet there must be a height to be reached, beyond things personal, from which it should be possible to contemplate the two events side by side with God-like calmness – a level of experience where the words ring true, "love thy neighbour as thyself", or even "love thine enemy". This is a level to which this exercise points, though it may seem far beyond our present capacity to achieve.

Yet the fruits of the first two exercises are with us. We are less fettered to our personality than we were before. When we have laid aside our personality in death, will we not be entering a world where quite other rules obtain? And what does it mean in spiritual life to die to oneself? Such an exercise, if faithfully pursued, cleanses one of excess self-love and egotism. We are membered in a third world through that in us which is the bearer of impulses, desires, passions, hopes and frustrations, that part in us which does, indeed, carry the dramatic struggle of our inner life. Anthroposophy speaks, in addition to a physical body and an etheric body, of an astral body (aster – a star), related to the world of the stars, in which, for example, the ancient Egyptians and other peoples could read what pertained to earthly human destiny. Through this third exercise we may learn to attain positive acceptance of our destiny whatever it may bring, and contemplate our trials with a measure of equanimity and even thankfulness.

Beyond the physical body, beyond the life or etheric body, beyond the desire or astral body, is the human ego of which these are the sheaths. The fourth exercise in this series relates to the human ego. The three bodies give shape and expression to the outer personality. The ego is the core of man's being; it is at one and the same time our innermost being and that in us which is all-human. Only an ego can know itself apart from all that surrounds it and establish conscious relationship with all. Only an ego can think. The fourth exercise has to do with thinking. It introduces us to the nature of meditation.

We select a thought that ranges beyond the personal and applies equally to all human beings, a thought that is born out of deep experience and carries the testimony of its own truth within it.

Such a thought might be: "The heights of the spirit can only be climbed by passing first through the portals of humility." We place such a thought in the centre of our consciousness and try again and again to immerse ourselves in it to the exclusion of all else. We do not cogitate it. In the stillness of our soul we strive to live it. For most of us this requires a great effort of will but the earlier exercises have already partly prepared us. There can come a time when the thought itself becomes a portal of entry to communion in thought, to communion in spirit with a world of beings. To quote Rudolf Steiner:

Thus he now shifts the central point of his being to the inner part of his nature. He listens to the voices within him, which speak to him, in his moments of tranquillity; he cultivates an intercourse with the spiritual world . . . . He discovers that something living expresses itself in his thought-world. He sees that his thoughts do not merely harbour shadow-pictures but that through them hidden beings speak to him. Formerly sound reached him only through his ear; now it resounds through his soul. An inner language, an inner world is revealed to him.

The four exercises have been so described as to give a first impression of the nature of anthroposophical inner work. As exercises, it will be seen, they are transparently clear. Yet because they are born of initiation knowledge, the order in which they occur is significant – thus, from the point of view from which they are given, they comprise a whole man. At the same time they provide a starting point for great truths still to be discovered. Through his four members, body, life, soul and spirit, man is related to four kingdoms of nature, the mineral, plant and animal and, in its own distinct character, the human kingdom.

But man is related to kingdoms above him. Nature, the divine in nature, has brought him to his present state of being. It now rests with him, in his freedom, to carry his evolution further. What we have presented so far has reference to the first part of *Knowledge of Higher Worlds*. That part ends with the following words: "Spiritual science gives the means of developing the spiritual eyes and ears, and kindling the spiritual light; the method of spiritual training may be described as consisting of three stages: *Probation:* this develops the spiritual senses. *Enlightenment:* this kindles the spiritual light. *Initiation:* this establishes intercourse with higher spiritual beings."

Stages of Initiation

These three stages have always existed in the mystery schools of the past though the conditions will have been different. The demands on the student deepen and increase as the work advances from stage to stage.

Again to take an example by way of illustration: The exercise laid out for the observation of the plant can carry a long way. But now, at a later stage, comes a further exercise; to bring one's attention to bear on the plant budding and blossoming, and then again, the plant wilting and withering. To help one, Rudolf Steiner compares the experience of the budding and blossoming to that of a sunrise; the wilting and withering not as one might expect to a sunset, but to the rising of the moon. A sunrise – a moonrise. Here is an instance to show that in spiritual matters one cannot rely on simple logic – the realities may call for quite different images. This exercise would lead to a heightened experience of all that is coming into being and passing away in nature – eventually to an awakening to the etheric world.

The following is an exercise which requires an even greater degree of concentration. The student has before him a seed and alongside the mere likeness of a seed. Whilst contemplating the seed, he may call up in imagination all the possible development that is there. Turning to the non-seed, he may experience intensely how by no stretch of imagination can anything be expected to arise there. It is important to have the objects before one – not merely think them in the abstract.

So we could pass on to an exercise contrasting the experience of a crystal in its form and expression to that of an animal driven hither and thither by desire and instinct, and then direct attention to a plant as holding an intermediary position between mineral and animal.

There are exercises to do with listening which bring into effect quite other faculties, to listen to a bell, for example, then to the cries and calls of an animal and then to the speech of a human being.

All these exercises call for clear thinking and strengthened feeling, for patient repetition, for the right quality of devotion, and the right degree of concentration.

The *seeing* exercises lead more towards imagination, the *listening* exercises towards inspiration. Intuition requires before all else the cultivation of love for the world and for all beings.

To make more clear what is meant by the greater freedom of the man of today, we might look briefly at an earlier time. Rudolf Steiner has described some of the mystery centres of the past.

It is hard to imagine how strictly guarded these mystery schools were from the public. To divulge any of their teachings merited death. Aeschylus was once in this danger but was able to prove his innocence. We will imagine we are in ancient Egypt. Someone approaches the temple gates. He wishes to enter as a pupil, a neophyte. He is met by a sage from within the temple, a hierophant or initiate. After a searching interview, instead of being admitted right away he may be advised to remain longer in the world outside, to exercise his natural gifts and qualities further, maybe to work for a time with the sick or the needy in some poor area, to explore what other unused capacities he might have; in any case to cultivate a regular devotional life, to establish an inner state of balance in thought and word and deed, especially in dealing with others, and then to come back. All this would have corresponded to what we have indicated as preliminary conditions.

Once entered, then a life of discipline awaits him under strict guidance. He is first admitted to the outer court only, where he is led through stringent tests and trials to cultivate higher vision – this would correspond to what we have called probation leading through a process of purification to conscious spiritual imagination. Then, when he is considered sufficiently prepared, it is decided by the ruling powers of the temple to admit him to the middle court, where even severer disciplines await him; where he may have to live through extremes of fear beyond anything normally known, and great enticements of soul (we may think of the temptations that Buddha underwent on the eve of enlightenment, or the trials and temptations of St. Anthony), this eventually leading to actual communion with divine beings, which we might call conscious spiritual inspiration. A long and even more arduous path awaits him before he can hope to merit entry into the innermost court, the holy of holies; he would have to experience the laying aside of his personality, eliminating the last trace of self-love, to all intents and purposes dying to himself in a death-sleep of three day duration – always under the immensely watchful and unremitting care of his initiate teachers. Such would be the path towards conscious spiritual intuition – a state of one-ness with the divine. He might then be called on to go back as a master into life, as a guide and teacher to his fellow men.

This brief sketch may show how the inner life of man conforms to eternal divine laws. Today the onus rests on each one to determine his own way. Anthroposophy opens a way which each may follow.

Even from his first teachings Rudolf Steiner is able to bring what concerns the very highest in man into forms which can be grasped, understood and practised in daily life. There is no question at any point of blind dependence, of placing one's will under the jurisdiction of another. These higher truths live germinally in all. From this point of view, let us glance once again at the terms imagination – living in images; inspiration, living through the word; intuition, discovering and uniting with being.

We meet someone for the first time. To begin with we have only an outer impression of the person, an image. The moment real conversation begins between us, things become very different. We reveal something of our being, the one to the other. The world comes to life between us. This is no longer mere image. If our communication is a true one, we inspire one another with new-found riches. We become friends. This friendship may grow and deepen until a genuine love grows up between us. We begin to know one another from within. That is also intuition, the capacity to enter into one another – this intuitive knowing from within is to love. Thus we see how these gifts that we bring towards one another are at the same time the incipient beginnings of what may grow and unfold into the three stages of higher consciousness: beholding, communing, divining. The seed forces for such a higher development are present in all of us.

Anthroposophy speaks of:

Conscious Imagination: beholding the world as image of the divine in its working and weaving.

Conscious Inspiration: communing with the divine, revelation of the Word in nature.

Conscious Intuition: growing to be one with the divine – in older language, becoming one with God.

These are the three stages implied by the words Probation, Enlightenment, Initiation.

We use the terms imagination, inspiration, intuition in referring to artists, poets, creative thinkers. We regard them quite truly as gifts welling up from unconscious depths, carrying experience beyond the mundane and commonplace. Before a great work of art we feel 'translated' as though raised to another level of being.

In anthroposophy these terms are employed to mean an actual awakening in full consciousness to those realms whence these experiences reach us, an awakening to the beings in higher worlds connected with human destiny and waiting for human beings to awaken to them for the greater well-being of the world as a whole: they have not relinquished us, though we in our materialistic age appear to have forgotten them.

The Basic Books

Anthroposophy offers various ways of approach to the question of inner development but they all meet in the one end goal, the awakening of man to his own true being and thereby also to the spiritual foundation of all existence.

What we have presented so far relates particularly to the first part of *Knowledge of Higher Worlds*, the part that was originally entitled *The Way of Initiation*. The second half, *Initiation and its Results*, seemingly offers a different approach but actually supplements and illuminates the first part. It is not a case of choosing the one way or the other. The student is entirely free to choose from each or both what appears to him to suit him best. The second part, like the first, follows a given order. It offers exercises for the shaping and perfecting of certain soul and spirit organs of perception even as nature has provided clearly shaped sense organs for cognizing the physical world. It goes on to describe resulting changes of consciousness first in dream life and then in waking life. We are led to the first full encounter with oneself in what is described as the meeting with the Guardian of the Threshold, and thence, eventually, to a meeting with the Greater Guardian at the threshold of death. We think of Odysseus crossing the river Styx to the realm of Hades to bring back from the dead new powers for the guidance of the living. Here again is an example of how Rudolf Steiner quite typically unfolds from the very beginning a view that carries through to the end so that, though we confront mysteries to be resolved, we never need feel left in the dark.

The book *Theosophy* is also an early work, 1904. (The name of the book has no connection with the Theosophical Society.) A man is walking across a meadow. He discovers a threefold relationship between himself and the world around him. First he views himself from outside simply as a body amongst bodies. Next he recalls his memories of that same meadow a year ago, compares his experiences then and now, and thus recognizes an inner life which belongs to him alone, and which, to begin with, may be called soul. But then, a student of botany, he explores and discovers the laws and conditions of plant life. The truths he discovers are equally true for all men. To this capacity to transcend the personal and achieve the universal may be assigned the name spirit. The recognition that man is a being of body and soul and spirit provides the ground plan for the whole book. This threefold nature is elaborated further into a sevenfold and even a ninefold man within the total evolutionary process. The description carries us beyond death, to the experiences the soul passes through in the soul world, the spirit in the spirit world. The laws of metamorphosis translate the past into a new future, in other words, are resolved into the laws of reincarnation. Man finds himself once more upon the earth. All he has lived through in body, soul and spirit is gathered up into a re-encounter with the circumstances of a new earthly existence. The book ends with still another way of approach to initiation.

Occult Science, an Outline, 1908, is the third and most comprehensive of the three basic books. *Knowledge of Higher Worlds* is concerned with individual development in the course of a single lifetime and *Theosophy* extends this to the shaping of human inter-relationships from lifetime to lifetime. *Occult Science,* whilst presenting anew their main contents, sets out to embrace the whole of human and world evolution, a vast but marvellously coherent description, yet still only an outline. We learn to see man not as a chance creature on this earth but as coeval with the universe that contains him. They are counterparts of each other, "Would'st know thyself, look into the world," says Rudolf Steiner, and the reverse, "Would'st know the world, look into thyself". The use of the word 'occult' in the title simply declares that what was once held concealed is now an open secret. It only remains hidden for the one who fails or is not willing to understand it.

As time went on many different aspects opened up; religion, the arts, the sciences and humanities, the social sciences, education, medicine, agriculture, and other practices. All of these contributed to the central theme of redeeming the image of man from its present fallen estate in matter and raising it to its true status of being as central to the whole evolutionary process.

Aspects of the Being of Man

Man in the Kingdoms of Nature

ANTHROPOSOPHY is concerned primarily with the understanding of man. There presents itself the immediate question of his relationship to the kingdoms around him, mineral, plant and animal. Darwin could foresee no bridge being built from mineral to plant, that is, from the nonliving to the living, or from plant to animal. He conceived the thought that man and ape must have had a common ancestor and that, therefore, there was no such sharp dividing line between animal and man – hence his *Origin of Species* and *Descent of Man*. So far the supposed 'missing link' between ape and man has evaded all search. Despite fossil finds since Darwin's day, no creature living or in the fossil past has been declared as the actual ancestor of modern man.

Teilhard de Chardin goes to great lengths in his *Phenomenon of Man* to show that *thinking* could not have been derived either from animal instinct or even from animal intelligence at its highest level. He concludes that the birth of thought in man can only be regarded as a special act of creation. Goethe saw man with his upright carriage and conscious life of striving as standing at the peak of nature so that in him nature itself is carried further in a manner human–divine into art, science, religion and human culture generally. Out of his immersion in the living processes of nature, confronting a Greek work of art, he could say, "This is necessity, this is God."

The ruling concept of today of physical continuity from the most elementary particle to the most highly evolved organism leaves no entry for the human spirit. Man continues to be regarded as an animal, a highly advanced animal, nay, even a thinking animal, but still an animal: animal cries are the precursors of the human word, animal instincts of human conduct and morality. In the world of orthodox science no higher concept of man has yet been admitted.

Anthroposophy makes a different approach. It reviews four basic phenomena which we all may recognize, namely, form, life, sentience (a consciousness based on sense-experience) and selfhood (an awareness of the self). It is these four primary phenomena we will need to consider, for all four remain unfathomable mysteries, (whatever theories may be propounded), in the modern fields of knowledge. As our point of departure we may say: *Form* man shares with mineral, plant, and animal. *Life* man shares with plant and animal. *Sensory experience* man shares with animal (instincts, desires, joy and pain, etc.) *Thinking*, that is, a reflective consciousness, an inborn sense of self or the I AM man alone, in the world of nature, possesses.

Anthroposophy, in exploring new ways into the future also pays high regard to what lived as ruling wisdom in the past and has since been forgotten. It therefore turns its attention to the four classical elements which played such a big rôle in earlier times right back to ancient India as we will endeavour to show later, but here we will turn specially to ancient Greece. (A feeling for the four elements lived on through the Middle Ages.) We refer to the four elements, Earth, Water, Air and Fire.

It so happened that during a formal inspection of Michael Hall School in Forest Row (the first English-speaking Rudolf Steiner school) the science inspector came across these terms in a child's notebook. He wanted to know how such 'Aristotelian terms' had found their way into a science notebook. The teacher tried to explain that in his understanding these terms were not to be taken in their merely physical meaning. He regarded them, rather, as relating to dynamic powers working through the whole of nature; that is how he understood them to have been regarded in Greek times, not only by Aristotle. The kind of thinking which could take hold of the mineral kingdom was not adequate for the plant kingdom, nor thoughts for the plant kingdom for the animal kingdom, nor could thoughts related to animals be adequate for the comprehension of man. These four dynamics in nature called for discriminating qualities in human thinking and it was to demonstrate this that the teacher had introduced these classical terms. They were the best he could find. The inspector, after a silent pause, said he thought he understood though he would probably not have used the word, 'dynamics'. This is quoted here to show that to an open mind the approach, one might even say, the rediscovery of these four elements, can be full of suggestive meaning. That inspector was an exceptionally open-minded person on other counts as well.

But to return now to our main exposition. With the term 'Earth' can be associated the individualizing power that manifests in all the multitudinous distinctly recognizable forms in the mineral, plant and animal kingdoms, and also in the human kingdom where every individual person carries his own distinct identity.

Every *form* as we perceive it has been engendered in the first place out of 'water' or the fluid element which itself, at most, has only the form of a drop. The globe of the earth is such a drop in which there float the mineral masses.

Crystals come into form and even grow in a medium of water. However, when 'water' in its dynamic character penetrates 'earth' as it does in the plant, then we arrive at forms endowed with life. There is an unfolding of form from within outwards. We may say, in the plant the water has become an inner principle – it has become the bearer of life. Whatever is living owes its life to the active presence of water. Man is far more 'water' than he is 'earth'.

In the plant, then, we see earth penetrated by water, form combined with life.

The plants live in a medium of surrounding air and warmth.

When air penetrates living nature as an inner principle, the rhythmic process of respiration arises and with it the birth of sensory nature – animal nature is born. The more penetrating the airy process, the more highly are the senses developed, and with them the nervous system. We need only compare, let us say, a fish with a bird. Nerve, circulation, metabolism, take their measure from the breath. In the invertebrate the balance of these has a different character but it is still the penetration of the element air that is determinative. Anima can be translated as breath.

In the animal then, we have the three elements earth, water, air, giving rise to form imbued with life, and endowed with sensory experience or soul. The surrounding medium not yet incorporated fully is the element of 'warmth' (fire).

When warmth penetrates the threefoldness of earth, water and air as an inner principle, then, at the highest level of animal the warm-blooded creatures arise, namely birds, mammals and also man. By warm-blooded is meant the capacity of the creature to engender warmth as required and to regulate it to meet varying conditions, winter and summer. This the bird can do, but the reptile can not – hence the reptile and creatures below it are called cold-blooded. Reptiles go into a coma with cold and into a torpor with heat, in both cases suffering a subduing of consciousness. With the inwardizing of warmth social features appear, in the care of the young, in bird calls, in animal calls.

But now, in man, this inner warmth takes on a totally new dimension, that of conscious love, a life in ideals to the point of sacrifice, devotion to the highest, new creations beyond the bounds of nature: the element of 'fire' in nature transmutes in man into spiritual fire, and creative endeavour.

We see man surrounded by the mineral, plant and animal kingdoms, yet in his innermost being standing within his own kingdom which leads him out of bondage to nature towards the realization of the divine. He gazes out at nature, responsive and responsible, yet able to iterate the words: "my kingdom is not of this world."

The Human Being in Himself

Man is a being who can look both outwards and inwards. Looking outwards he beholds the world of nature and himself as part of that world. Looking inwards he beholds himself in his thinking, feeling and willing. The world around him conforms to certain laws and conditions. Changes in the order of things can be traced to outer causes. Man, too, is subject to these laws and conditions. In his life of thinking, feeling and willing, however, he carries his own law within him out of which to direct his life.

Ideally he should be master of himself, actually he is only partly so. His thoughts can run away with him. His feelings can rise up unbidden. To maintain a clear line of thought is not always easy. To maintain an even command of feeling is mostly difficult. Compared with thought and feeling our will remains dark to us unless roused to action. We can be driven to act on the spur of the moment and then are left to reflect on the consequences. On the other hand an impulse can light up as a sudden thought, even as a flash of genius.

Both instincts and intuitions rise up from the hidden depths of will. They should not be confused; the former come with compulsive force, the latter as guiding messages. Sometimes the will pervades the life of feeling unaccountably with a sense of expectancy, or maybe with foreboding as though anticipatory of some future.

All this belongs to the inner drama of the life of the soul playing between the light of thought and the stirrings of

will with the life of feeling mediating between them, lend-
ing colour to a thought, or itself aglow and afire with a
prompting of will. There is a Greek image of a charioteer
having to keep under control three horses, all at the same
time. Thinking, feeling, and willing are the three horses.

In the normal course of life we are awake by day, asleep
by night, with the dream arising between. There comes the
question however, how far we are truly awake in the day. A
little consideration will show that we are really fully awake
only in our thinking. We can be so absorbed in thought as
to grow oblivious to what is going on around us. As an
inexperienced driver we have to keep our thoughts concen-
trated on every detail of what we are doing; later we may
drive with a minimum of thought, simply out of habit,
whilst our mind is mainly engaged elsewhere. In so simple
an action as picking up a pencil to write something down,
we obviously need to think on what we are doing, but, as
regards the actual doing, apart from calling the will into
action, in its own nature it remains completely hidden from
us. In recalling the events of a day, only what we have
observed consciously in thought stand out clearly for us.
Some things we recall in a kind of haze and a great deal has
passed us by completely for we were simply not awake to it.
We thus confront the fact that even in our waking day, we
are in part awake, in part adream, and in part asleep. We are
awake in our thinking, we are adream in our feeling, but as
regards our will, we are as asleep to it by day as we are by
night. Yet these three faculties of thinking, feeling and
willing are for ever interacting. We could not exercise our
thinking were there not some element of will present, nor
could we reach down to grasp an intuition of will without
the light of our thinking directed to it. Feeling is always in
some measure playing in.

This threefold nature of thinking, feeling and willing
related to waking, dreaming and sleeping is one aspect of
our inner life. There is another connected with the quality

of consciousness with which we apprehend life itself. We may distinguish four such qualities, intellectual, imaginative, inspirational, and intuitive.

Through the force of intellect we become immediately cognizant of the world as it first meets us.

Where feeling enters into our perceptual faculty as was the case with Goethe, we pass from external knowledge to insight: not only the thinker but also the artist in us is born. We, with imagination, enter *into* the phenomena we behold. The visual arts, painting and sculpture, lead us on the way to imagination. Feeling, however, enters into all the arts. Music is a 'hearing' art. A musician can hear tones that reach beyond the ear. We need only think of Beethoven who never heard the greatness of his music as others do, yet who drew that music from a source. All true music sounds into the world out of what Pythagoras described as the harmony of the spheres. Here we come closer to the faculty of inspiration.

There is a listening beyond the silence which poets also know. Poetry, the art of the word, belongs to what is innermost in us, 'In the beginning was the Word.' It carries us towards the realm of intuition where we become one with Being.

There is no question here of framing categories but of recognizing these different qualities, each with its own significance in human life. The works of architects, sculptors, painters, also speak to us. There are musicians who are descriptive and imaginative. One might say that amongst English poets Keats lived more in the quality of imagination, Shelley in that of inspiration, and Wordsworth in intuition, but clearly all three qualities lived in each of them and each, in his art, gave birth to profound thoughts. Anthroposophy can lead us to see how each of the four qualities of consciousness, as we have described them, has its particular seat within the total nature of man.

To reduce experience to thought forms in intellectual life

becomes possible because man possesses a physical organ, the brain, as an instrument. The brain, in its perfect formation within the physical body, relates to the element 'Earth'.

The faculty of imagination rests in equal measure upon the ever flowing, ever shaping and renewing quality of 'Water' in which is reflected the life body or etheric body.

Inspiration relates to the breath, to the inbreathing and outbreathing, the toning and intoning of the astral body, resting in earthly life upon the element 'Air'.

The life of intuition finds its ground in the creative fire force within us, the ego dwelling in the element of 'Warmth'.

Combining this with what has gone before we can conclude the summary as follows:

Earth	_Water_	_Air_	_Fire_
Physical body	Etheric body	Astral or Soul body	Ego
Intellectual faculty	Imaginative faculty	Inspirational faculty	Intuitive faculty

The Threefold Human Organism

In 1917, after thirty years of spiritual-scientific research, as he himself tells us, Rudolf Steiner first gave out his description of the threefold organism. He describes how the body consists of three distinct though closely related organizations, a nerve-sense system centred in the head, a rhythmic-circulatory system centred in the chest, and a limb-metabolic system centred in the abdomen. These three systems are co-active in every part of the body: where there is nerve there is blood, and along with the blood, respiration and metabolism. They represent three different principles: the nerve-sense system comprising brain, nerves and senses is related to the conscious life of thought; the rhythmic-circulatory system comprising lung, heart and circulation as the centre of the rhythmic functioning of the body to the life of feeling; and the limb-metabolic system (limb and metabolism being inseparable in their functioning) to the life of will.

Through these three systems man stands in three relationships to his environment. In the head he receives sense impressions and gives out his answering thoughts as described earlier. In the chest he takes in oxygen and gives back the carbon dioxide produced by his body. In his abdomen, the seat of the digestive process, he takes in the foodstuffs which he reduces to solubility, passes them through the intestinal walls by a process of absorption, and the resulting lymph is then carried into the blood for the further process of assimilation: thus there is catabolism or the breaking down of the substances of outer nature, and anabolism, the corresponding building up of substances within the organism, processes which science can record but can by no means explain in physical terms alone. In the head we engage in the world process through the refined nature of our sense perceptions, in the chest through the rare element of air, in the abdomen through the heavier elements of water and earth, here using the term 'elements' as introduced earlier. There is thus intensification in terms of substance process from the head down, and accentuation in consciousness process from below up. In the head, the consciousness pole, metabolism is most reduced; in the abdomen where metabolism is at its intensest, consciousness is most dimmed down. In the middle system, the rhythmic-circulatory, we oscillate between enhanced consciousness on the in breathing and a diminution of consciousness on the out breathing. We enter earthly life on the first inbreath and leave the world again on the last outbreath.

The interplay of the three soul forces of thinking, feeling and willing via the threefold bodily organism has been closely studied since it was first made known in 1917. It plays greatly into the practice of education, medicine, the social sciences, and many other aspects of man's relationship to the world he is in. It is understandable that this view of the three-fold organism is highly challenging to much of modern theory but, as we have already indicated, modern outlook includes a great deal of questioning of the present state of knowledge, and the awakening of many people, not least amongst scientists, to a sense that there are new boundaries to be crossed. It is very much a question of the way of approach to these matters. There is no likelihood of progress so long as one persists in the view that man is no more than the material body perceptible to the physical senses.

At a recent conference convened by young people of seventeen to nineteen, approaching the end of their schooling or having recently left, the question was brought forward, 'How are we to understand such terms as material and spiritual?' Since these two terms are loaded with ambiguities and possible misconceptions, a different way of approach to the question was offered by substituting for material and spiritual the terms, sensible and supersensible. By sensible we mean everything accessible to the senses – that is quite clear. But now, turning to man, he lives by his thoughts, his feelings, his will. Thinking or thoughts are not accessible to the senses, yet we are fully aware of them – they are beyond sense-experience, super-sensible. So are feelings and so is the will super-sensible. Thus man, as regards his inner life, is a super-sensible being. What we see of him with the senses belongs to the material world. What, then, of what we do not see with the senses? It is possible to develop the inner faculties by an inner schooling, then man can grow aware that, just as in his physical body he belongs to the material world, the world of the senses, so through his supersensible nature he belongs to a supersensible world of supersensible facts and beings. That is what the great teachers of humanity were able to reach. By an inner schooling, a heightening of the faculties they possessed as thinking, feeling and willing, they raised themselves to higher worlds. As spiritual teachers they did not theorize, they bore witness to the spirit. Once we begin to recognize that man, as regards his inner life is a super-sensible being, all that remains is to train this further. But there is one condition, that man should train the faculties he already possesses in order to acquire true knowledge and understanding of the world of the senses. This is essential as preparation for a higher seeing and knowing later. The young people felt they had been well served – they could relate to the terms sensible, supersensible, in a way they could work with.

In regard to the understanding of the functioning of the threefold organism, there are obstacles to be overcome. One is the misconception that *all* human experience, thinking, feeling, and willing, is centred, controlled and directed by the head, meaning the brain. The brain as an organ is most perfectly formed and marvellously related to the organism as a whole, but in itself it is the most effete, having less recuperative power and vitality than any organ in the body. In so far as thinking is an activity, a function of will, it cannot originate in the brain. Rudolf Steiner likens the brain to a mirror; it reflects what is otherwise life and impulse and action in the form of abstract thoughts, mirror images without substance. Only if we bring will and feeling into these shadow thoughts do they take on a life, become *living* thoughts with which to take hold of reality. We see in the world today how ineffectual is abstract thinking, unable to grasp and enter into what is really calling; thus we are drowned in questions which remain unanswered and lead to frustration and violent protest. It is soul and spirit that are calling out of intuitive depths for consciousness to awaken out of the sleep of materialism.

Another immense challenge is to the idea that the heart is a pump. The real challenge lies in the lack of understanding of the true nature of blood, which continues to be regarded as a vegetative fluid. In fact it is the bearer of the warmth element, the fire in us. How this warmth or fire is generated, how maintained, how it enters the will and empowers the mind, are questions waiting to be answered. Blood is the most vital tissue in the body, so vital that it continues in a flowing state, this ever self-renewing blood through whose unceasing working all the organs and tissues of the body are constantly being renewed. Blood is the very antithesis of what Rudolf Steiner describes as the 'dying nerve'. It is the blood that appears in the embryo first; then comes the gradual forming of the heart by the blood which is ever flowing. The heart is created by the blood to serve the blood. Great problems to be solved by future science are involved here as in the question of the functioning of the brain.

And another basic error lives in the view that man is the continuation of the food he eats. Such a view, though not always expressed so crudely, ignores the hidden realities that underlie the three stages of digestion, absorption, and assimilation. It also ignores the amazing fact of what it is, in all this flux of continuous action of breaking down and building up, that faithfully maintains the image, the uniqueness of each single individual as member of the human race. For further consideration of the functioning of the threefold organism, the small book, *Living with your Body*, by Dr. Walther Bühler, can well be recommended.

The Child Growing

There can be no better way of perceiving the reality of the threefold nature of man than by following the process of the growing child. This declares itself already in the first three years of life.

The child at birth is the most helpless of creatures, utterly dependent on those who receive it. There it lies unable to lift its large head, its relatively small limbs making jerky, sporadic movements, its eyes in a voidless stare.

It takes weeks for its gaze to find a focus and with this comes its first smile of recognition, and at about the same time the appearance of a first actual tear. That first smile and tear is the beginning of human language, the first unmistakable mark of a human being.

As the weeks and months go by, we witness what are little short of a series of miracles. We see that child begin to crawl, a kind of first voyage of exploration into this world it has entered. We see it able to sit unaided. Within the space of a year we see this helpless infant, by its own tireless efforts, raise itself to the vertical. Only the human being can do this. There it stands upright between the above and the below; next, it establishes its balance from right to left, and within a short while it is taking its first step forwards. It is now master of the three dimensions of space. This is the achievement of the first year; the co-ordination and the mastery of bodily movements.

During that first year its language is one of gestures, but we hear it after the first few months in a remarkable fashion actually practising linguistic sounds. By the second year it has co-ordinated these sounds into the shaping of words. In the second year it begins to speak. This is no longer just physical, it belongs to the inward life of soul.

At the next stage, the child begins to co-ordinate words to shape a phrase, a sentence, carrying a mental image, a thought. It begins to approach a life of thought, of that which leads to a life transcending body and soul alone and to which we can ascribe spirit.

Yet now comes the crowning event of this earliest phase of childhood: there comes a moment when the child for the first time utters the word "I", and feels self-identified with that word for the whole of life. This is the birth of the ego, of the awareness of one's own self. Hence it marks also the birth of personal memory, the birth of an autobiography.

For those who are willing to perceive it, we have outlined

the sequence from gesture to word to thought, and then to the uniquely self-born thought of the "I". This we may also describe as a progression from body to soul to spirit, the three members of the human being, crowned by the ego, the I. We thus see how in the first three years we have the foreshadowing of a total human being. To enter into this is to recognise man already in relation to all that is round him as a special order of creation. Anthroposophy in its total exposition is primarily concerned with this.

The sequence as Rudolf Steiner described it, from gesture, to word, to thought – we could also say from limb, to heart, to head – finds a natural extension into the three phases of childhood: infancy, childhood proper and adolescence. On this were formerly based the three grades of schooling, infant school up to age six, elementary school up to fourteen and upper or high school up to eighteen, to be followed by the three years at college or in some other professional training. This has been changed in more recent times, mainly because of the tendency to push intellectual education down the years. The former division is still closely adhered to in the education founded by Rudolf Steiner, Waldorf education. The transition times are looked on as relating to the change of teeth and also puberty, physiological changes which also bring changes in the whole sequence of life and consciousness. This is dealt with more fully in the author's *Rudolf Steiner Education* and in other such books written out of teaching practice in Waldorf schools of which there are at present over four hundred spread through the world. In what follows here, only the broadest features are brought forward in so far as they provide a basis for the further study of the threefold man.

Teacher and Child

It has been long acknowledged that the human physical body is replaced every seven years. This involves an adjustment of the whole being in body, soul and spirit, which is most markedly the case in the three successive phases of childhood. The attitude of the teacher and the type of teaching varies accordingly. That this should be so is strongly cultivated in Waldorf schools everywhere.

In the first seven years, the imitative years, the most decisive factor is what the adult is, not only in outer demeanour and behaviour but in inner attitude to life. The unconscious ideal of early childhood, says Rudolf Steiner, is that the world is built on goodness. Thus the teacher in the kindergarten needs to meet the children with devotion of heart born of a religious attitude to life. This will then flow towards all that the children do, for education in these imitative years is achieved through *doing*. All the child does in drawing, painting, making, movement, is an exercise in doing the good.

For the eight years of the elementary school, the situation is quite different. The ideal underlying childhood in this time is that the world is built on harmony and beauty. The teacher needs to be an artist. His medium is the written and spoken word through which he portrays what he has to give, both of man and nature, in an imaginative form that reaches the feelings and therefore the hearts of the children. They cease to imitate outwardly but identify themselves with the pictures and descriptions thus offered which, together with the art they do, truly becomes 'a heart education'. We see the wisdom of this progression from infancy to puberty being under the aegis of a class teacher who moves forward with his/her group of children from year to year, who maintains the continuity of the main teaching and at the same time co-ordinates what the other teachers bring to that same group of children fulfilling, as far as is possible, the conditions of a work of art where all elements are in harmonious relationship with one another.

Then, what is achieved in the learning by doing – the limb-learning we might call it of the early years and the heart-learning of the middle years – flows into the upper or high school years where the ideal of the adolescent is that the world is built on truth. Here the work rests with specialist teachers, each one making a case for his particular subject, be it in the sciences, the humanities, the arts and also in the most important theme of social evolution from ancient times down to today. Education thus acquires meaning for life and offers a sense of direction for the social future.

Man in a Threefold Society

At the time of the French Revolution a call sounded forth, the call of Liberty, Equality, Fraternity. Rudolf Steiner, during the calamitous years of the First World War, brought forward, as though in answer to that call, his ideas for a Threefold Commonwealth. The picture of the Three-fold Commonwealth runs directly parallel to that of the threefold nature of man as we have tried to describe it. His ideas could not be realized, and though they have given rise to study and research, and to a few modest enterprises, they remain ideas or ideals for the future. What mainly militates against them, and is likely to do so for some time to come, is the centralist trend in thought that is ever looking for head leadership whether by individuals or through party control. Such leadership will naturally tend to direct development after its own pattern in political, in economic, in educational and in cultural life. This century has seen a striking rise in dictatorship states, the goal proclaimed always being that of ultimate freedom. That the call for freedom has a genuine inner source in human beings today can scarcely be questioned. Yet in practice we find ourselves under pressure of increasing unfreedom. Reverting to the original call we ask, where does freedom or liberty truly reside, where do we expect to find equality, and though the term fraternity or brotherhood is often heard, what does it signify and where do we meet it?

Where are we to look for liberty? Essentially in the sphere of thought. We would expect every individual to be entirely free to think his own thoughts, to worship in his own style, to pursue his own cultural interest, in fact, to conduct his own cultural life untroubled and untrammeled by any question of outer control.

Where shall we seek and expect to find equality? Most surely before the law. Justice belongs equally to all, before humanity and before God. That is beyond dispute. But then comes the question, what rightly belongs to humanity, what constitutes human rights? Everyone has a right to the air he breathes, to the water he drinks, (why not to the bread he eats?), to education in childhood, to medical service at need, to care in old age. Whatever one might claim as rights for oneself, one would surely do in the same spirit for one's neighbour. Is it not here in the sphere of rights, that the democratic principle is paramount? This is not the same idea as a welfare state administered from above. Rights and justice belong to the sphere of the heart, and the rulings here should spring from the heart in the mutual concern of men for one another.

What then is to be understood by fraternity or brotherhood? One often hears the word, but where does it really live? Here we are on more difficult ground. Fraternity springs from the gifts we bring towards one another in the services we render for one another. This directly engages the question of work and what we mean by economic life. It is quite clear that economic and industrial life need expert leadership, but in so far as they are there not for personal gain but in service to the community on the basis of meeting actual needs, their jurisdiction involves the sphere of rights. Here things get too complex for a cursory statement. We would quote as a concrete example that Henry Adams saw as a primary evil of economic life the personal ownership of land, and along with this, any form of land speculation. Our modern life is rife with it. The corrective view would be that land should be loaned by decision of the rights sphere to those deemed competent to make the best productive use of it for the common good.

Another example might be the following: the author was once asked to speak on the occasion of the opening of a new school of commerce. He stressed one particular point. In purchasing a pair of shoes, we pay for the commodity; but there is no way we can pay for the gift which enabled someone to make us shoes for our feet. We cannot traffic in human gifts, buy and sell labour, for gifts we bring with us into the world; gifts belong to the spirit; we could say, they are of God. A man should labour, not for money, but in order to fulfil himself in his service through his gifts to others, as they, through their gifts serve him. He works to sustain his fellow men even as they work to sustain him. That is how we are indebted to one another. But human needs should be a concern of the rights sphere. To work for wages determined by an employer is a form of slavery. Not to work or have the will to work except in illness or old age is an illness in itself, actually an evil. Not to be able to find work points to a sickness in society, an even greater evil. At every point in economic life we touch the sphere of morality and there fraternity arises. We admit all this is difficult. It is mentioned here as something which stands before us as a great challenge to be met, the whole question of work, wages and money.

For the present, to sum up we may say:

Liberty of thought relates to the nerve sense system, and belongs to the cultural sphere.

Equality relates to the heart and the rhythmic system and belongs to the rights sphere.

Fraternity concerns work, production and consumption, is related to the human will and the metabolic-limb system, and belongs to the economic sphere.

Just as we live through thought, feeling, and will in all three parts of the total organism, so does each one play his part in all three spheres of the social organism. The threefold man enters naturally into this picture of a threefold society. There need be no centralist rulership but instead a striving for a healthy inter-working of all three spheres, mutually related as are the three organizations within the total single organism.

SUMMARY

thinking	*feeling*	*will*
nerve-sense organization	rhythmic–circulatory organization	limb–metabolism organization
cultural sphere	rights sphere	economic sphere
Liberty	Equality	Fraternity

The subject of 'man in society' can be studied from various aspects. The foregoing, growing out of the preceding descriptions, offers one such approach.

Entry into a New Age of Light

The Age of Darkness: Kali-yuga

ANCIENT TEACHINGS tell of a Golden Age, Krita-yuga (20,000 years), a Silver Age, Treta-yuga (15,000 years), a Bronze Age, Dvapara-yuga (10,000 years), and a Dark or Iron Age, Kali-yuga (5,000 years).

This succession of the Ages is the oriental image of the Fall, a long, protracted process of separation from the Gods, in contrast to the sudden, cataclysmic event as described in the Bible. The dates given for Kali-yuga, confirmed by Rudolf Steiner, are 3101 BC to 1899 AD.

It is difficult to reconcile these dates with what we know of the depth and grandeur of Egyptian culture, the wonder and the beauty of Greek culture, the birth of civil law and citizenship in Roman times, and the rise and spread of Christianity right through the Middle Ages. It is a remarkable fact though that the invention of writing in Egypt came just about the time when Kali-yuga was approaching, about 3300 BC. Until that time all culture rested on memory and the spoken word.

The succession of ages from Golden to Silver to Bronze to Iron may be taken as symbolic of the transition in consciousness from intuition to inspiration to imagination, and then to the birth of the intellectual faculty with which man finds himself contemplating the world from outside, no longer able to find entry into it. The way to the spirit continued to be cultivated in the mystery schools for the guidance of the peoples, but for human beings generally direct experience of higher worlds became ever more obscured.

We need only compare the vivid portrayal of the life after death in the Egyptian *Book of the Dead* with the dim and shadowy Hades of the Greeks. Study confirms that with every advance in outer culture there is a corresponding diminution in active participation in the life of the spirit. In this way human experience has become more and more externalized. This reached its culmination in the nineteenth century with the advance of science and technology and, in the western world where this was taking place, the spread of scepticism with regard to any kind of spiritual existence.

In the case of Christianity, for example, one might have expected that two thousand years after the coming of Christ the world would have grown increasingly alive to what, if it has any meaning at all, must be regarded as the greatest of all Mysteries, a God become man, to live with man on earth, to die a human death, in order to overcome death for man's sake. As we look down the centuries in the Christian west, what do we find?

To begin with there were those who could bear direct witness to the life of Christ Jesus, his death and resurrection. Then came the witnesses of the witnesses and their witnesses by oral tradition. As this weakened it was succeeded by religious faith — men no longer knew but they believed on faith. Faith, as time went on, hardened into dogma. Then came a war of conflicting interpretations, and persecutions followed and heresy hunting. Then, with the advent of science, doubts arose leading to the scepticism we know.

We recall the 19th century book, *The Life of Jesus*, by Ernest Renan, written in all honesty, and, as he believed, with good intent. He sets aside all regard for the divinity of Christ and cannot sufficiently extol the man Jesus – the simple man of Nazareth. He goes so far as to persuade himself, and through his book to persuade others, that the miracles and the resurrection were tales foisted on to the people by Jesus' followers to impress them with his greatness – strange to what extremes mistaken honesty can go.

It led on, however, to the view, the heavens having been abolished, that henceforth morality, in so far as it exists, is to be sought for only in man, and that man must now come to terms with himself. We meet with the free-thinking nineteenth century individualist, his words expressed in the statement, 'I hold myself responsible for thought and word and deed to myself and none other.' Historically it amounts to a declaration of moral and spiritual independence, subscribed to, also, by the pioneering scientists of that time – in itself an admirable point of departure for a new beginning. So much for the course of faith in the new scientific age.

Taking a brief glance at Christian art, selecting just a few examples, we pass from the cosmic, the lofty grandeur of a Cimabue madonna, with a golden background of sun-filled heavenly glory, to a Fra Angelico for whom the angel world was still immediately present for man, then the great masters of the Renaissance who brought about, in Christian form, all the perfection of classical times, and then to all the tenderness and grace of a very human Murillo madonna, or to the stern announcement of the new man in a Rembrandt. Then we sink away into naturalism but still for a time with the glow of the artist's sensitivity. It became impossible to cope further with a madonna figure. Man does indeed find himself confronting the world alone with himself – if anything new is to come it can only be out of the resources of his own nature – new explorations open which break with all tradition. For example some would say that Turner was the master pioneer into a new life in colour.

Science also began out of a more philosophic regard for nature. It moved from natural philosophy to natural history, and the word, science, came later. But then, as we have seen, science chose to confine itself strictly to what the senses could offer, and to theorizing about its limited data. Eventually, amongst other discoveries of the 19th century, came the spectroscope, the evidence of which, combined with Newton's law of universal gravitation, led to the view that the whole visible universe was little more than an extension of the conditions found on earth. Man, himself, then, also came to be regarded as a product of the earth.

As a symptom of the times we quote another interesting book, *Religion without Revelation*, by Julian Huxley, a prominent biologist. In this book Huxley explains away the Christian Trinity in what to him are the simplest terms. We are all children of nature. He identified nature with the Father. We all have flashes of inspiration from time to time. This he takes as evidence that the evolving substance, protoplasm, still has life in it. These flashes represent what is otherwise described as illumination through the Holy Spirit. There is then the third element, the capacity to relate the substance he owes to nature to the ideas that light up in him; to relate substance and idea, Father and Holy Spirit, this mediating element without which there could be no progress, he regards as that which the Christians ascribe to Christ.

Huxley must be regarded as a serious, competent, and honest thinker; but he has no use for any kind of personalized religion, he finds no ground in himself for considering a world beyond the senses. As a biologist he concluded that if there is to be further evolution on earth it can only be through man, but man must have the will to make progress, must strive to realize the best ideas he has, hence his phrase, "Evolution has grown conscious," an idea which the most pious religionist would happily share with him. He retained his faith in the potentials of the human being but saw that if man had nothing to strive for he must sink into apathy or despair and thus he came himself to build up something akin to religion, or at least an ethics, in his Humanism. We have quoted Huxley because of his uncompromising attitude where truth is concerned, and yet seemingly from his youth on, extreme reluctance and total inability to entertain any kind of thought that goes beyond the physical. He is important for he stands as evidence for a frame of mind which only our age could have produced. It poses the question: what could be the next step?

C. E. M. Joad, a teacher of philosophy early in this century, wrote *Guide to Modern Thought*. In it he gives a broad and impartial survey of the main trends of thought projected into this century. At one point he speaks of three dethronements: the dethronement through Copernicus of the earth from its central place in the heavens; the dethronement through Darwin of man on his planet earth; and the dethronement through behaviourist psychology of mind in man.

This still holds, and we may well ask what has been enthroned instead. With all the heavy trials this century has gone through, human life has been shaken through and through. The future continues uncertain and immensely threatening, and hope of outer stability is at a far remove. All this has brought about a stirring of souls and the awakening to a need to find inner stability if real answers to the questions that come crowding in are to be found.

Rudolf Steiner, fully knowing and wishing to serve the positive values to be found in science, foresaw in all clarity that, with the end of Kali-yuga, a new light must dawn for humanity. Into what seems externally like darkness deepening, he was called on to bring anthroposophy, a new knowledge of man and world and human destiny, a knowledge brought in a form that makes it openly accessible. It comes as a source of new illumination from within, casting its light into all fields of new endeavour, and opening up perspectives of hope for the future.

The Initiate Teacher in the Age of Freedom

An important question will almost certainly have arisen in the mind of the reader: Do we have to take what Rudolf Steiner gives out as fruits of his spiritual investigation simply on trust? Lacking his capacity and his spiritual vision, how are we to verify for ourselves the truths of which he speaks? The answer to this question can best be given in his own words: "I have often said that the facts of the spiritual world must be investigated and can be discovered only by clairvoyant consciousness; and I have often said that once someone possessed of clairvoyant consciousness has observed these facts in the spiritual world and then communicates them, they must be communicated in such a way that even without clairvoyance everyone will be able to test them by reference to the normal feeling for truth present in every soul, and by applying to them his own unprejudiced reasoning faculties. Anyone endowed with genuine clairvoyant consciousness will always communicate the facts about the spiritual world in such a way that everyone who wishes to test what he says will be able to do so without clairvoyance. But at the same time. he will communicate them in a form whereby their true value and significance can be conveyed to a human soul."

Here, something may be interposed. Rudolf Steiner speaks in many places of the need for serious study of the content of what is given out by anthroposophy as basic to any other inner work that one might undertake. Such study is often found not easy for we encounter inevitably in ourselves all the misconceptions and limitations of a materialistic age which have been built into us from our earliest years. To these we are unconsciously so habituated that it can be hard work to recognize them for what they are and to eliminate them. We will find we cannot read books on spiritual science in the same way as we read other books and still hope to benefit from them. We need so to read as to dwell on each phrase and sentence, awaiting the right feelings to meet the thoughts. Then such study will serve as an awakener, for that is what spiritual science or anthroposophy is intended to be: to enable the human being to awaken truly to himself.

Reading in this way, we may come to realize that what is offered us in the book is the one half, in order that we may awaken the other half from within ourselves in response. This becomes a real need – the inwardizing of what we read and bringing it to life in ourselves. It is a common experience that re-reading something we have studied in this way, it lights up for us anew almost as a discovery of our own. Thus confidence grows.

Rudolf Steiner:

What, then, does this communication and presentation of spiritual facts mean to the soul? It means that anyone who has some idea of conditions in the spiritual world can direct and order his life, his thoughts, his feelings and his perceptions in accordance with his relationship to the spiritual world. In this sense, every communication of spiritual facts is important, even if the recipient cannot himself investigate these facts with clairvoyant consciousness. Indeed, for the investigator himself these facts acquire a human value only when he has clothed them in a form in which they can be accessible to everyone. However much a clairvoyant may be able to see and investigate in the spiritual world, it remains valueless both for himself and to others until he can bring the fruits of his vision into the range of ordinary cognition and express them in ideas and concepts which can be grasped by a natural sense of truth and by sound reasoning.

There is all the difference in the world between the spiritual investigator who pursues and tests his higher experiences in the true spirit of scientific research and the visionary whose impressions arise as and when they will. The Irish poet A. E. lamented the fact, at the end of his life, that he had never followed up a disciplined path of meditation. We have instances when Rudolf Steiner had to wait a long time, pursuing many avenues of research, before what he was looking for might suddenly reveal itself, often where least expected. .Such was the case in his search for the Grail. The answer to his search then came as an act of grace. Even so, having made his discovery and solved his problem for himself, he still had to wait until the conditions were appropriate and the right people present for communication of his findings to others. Hence his words: "In fact, if the findings are to be of any value to himself he must first have understood them fundamentally; their value begins where the possibility of reasoned proof begins." Only then, as he said previously, do the fruits of his work become accessible to the reasoned thinking of others, and only then can they be assimilated in freedom.

This whole question of the imparting of knowledge by the initiate to others Rudolf Steiner carries even to considerations beyond death.

Picture to yourselves a man who may have made quite exceptional discoveries in the spiritual world through clairvoyant observation but has never clothed them in the language of ordinary life. What happens to such a man? All his discoveries are extinguished after death; only so much remains of value and significance as has been translated into language which, in any given period, is the language of a healthy sense of truth.

But what is the obligation placed upon the spiritual investigator to communicate at all? Much may be at stake as to whether he does so or not. Supposing it is revealed to the spiritual investigator that humanity, in its state of ignorance, is in some great danger, is he not called on by everything holy to share what he can with his fellow human beings so that they may be rightly made aware? Here there is no compulsion, only compassion.

It is naturally of the greatest importance that clairvoyants should be able to bring tidings from the spiritual world and make them fruitful for their fellow-men. Our age needs such wisdom and cannot make progress without it. It is essential that such communications should be made available to contemporary culture. Even if this is not recognized today [1910] in fifty or a hundred years it will be universally acknowledged that civilization and culture can make no progress unless men become convinced of the existence of spiritual wisdom and realize that humanity must die unless spiritual wisdom is assimilated. And even if all space were conquered for the purpose of inter-communication, mankind would still have to face the prospect of the death of culture if spiritual wisdom were rejected. This is true beyond the shadow of doubt. Insight into the spiritual world is absolutely essential.

Referring once again to the state after death, the question is raised whether the initiate has, in fact, any advantage over someone who can only learn the truths from others. The answer comes very clear. What matters above all is to possess the right knowledge whereby to guide one's life on earth; if one has received such knowledge and has lived by it, then that alone is what is conclusive after death. "Whatever spiritual wisdom we have assimilated will be fruitful after death, no matter whether or not we ourselves are seers."

This is a great moral law.

Let nobody imagine that he (the seer) gains any advantage over his fellow-men through developing clairvoyance for that is simply not so. He makes no progress which can be justified on any ground of self-interest. He achieves progress only in so far as he can be more useful to others. The immorality of egoism can find no place in the spiritual world. A man can gain nothing for himself by spiritual illuminations. What he does gain, he can gain only as a servant of the world in general and he gains it for himself only by gaining it for others.[1]

Thus, in the spiritual world only truth prevails and Rudolf Steiner assumed that the sense for truth is in all men.

Age of Light

Rudolf Steiner left behind a great heritage of material, about thirty written works and over six thousand lectures.

Concerning the lectures he writes: "These were really reports on lectures, more or less accurate, which, for lack of time, I could not correct. It would have pleased me best if spoken words had remained spoken words." He had to yield to the pressure of members. At first the lectures were printed privately 'for members only', but the restriction had later to be dropped for it led to many misunderstandings.

It may be added that there is now a complete authentic and definitive edition of the lectures running to something like three hundred volumes.

About his writings, Rudolf Steiner comments:

Whoever wishes to trace my inner struggle to set anthroposophy before the consciousness of the present age must do this on the basis of the writings published for general circulation. Moreover, in these writings I make my position clear with respect to everything in the nature of a striving for knowledge, which exists in the present age.

And further:

Here is presented that which took form for me more and more in "spiritual beholding", what became the edifice of anthroposophy – in a form incomplete, to be sure, from many points of view.

It was the task of Rudolf Steiner, as a modern initiate of

[1] *On the Investigation and Communication of Spiritual Truths.* Lecture, Berlin 17 October 1910.

the west, to open the way for humanity out of Kali-yuga to a new age of light. Beginning with the periodical *Lucifer-Gnosis* he steadily built up his work offering a path through an exact study of natural phenomena to the spiritual facts and realities underlying them. It was for this task that his own studies and research in the nineteenth century had particularly prepared him. His work had to reach not only the open-minded thinking of the trained scientist, but a whole age brought up to be scientifically minded. His writing especially had to be framed for this, hence he writes:

. . . an anthroposophical book is designed to be taken up in inner experience. Then, by stages, a form of understanding comes about. The further deepening through exercises described in *Knowledge of Higher Worlds* is simply a confirmatory deepening. For progress on the spiritual road this is necessary; but a rightly composed anthroposophical book should be an awakener of the life of the spirit in the reader, not a certain quantity of information imparted. The reading of it should not be mere reading; it should be an experience with inner shocks, tensions and solutions.

At the same time, for freedom's sake he had to obtrude on the reader as little as possible, so much so that it has been said at times that his writing seems to be cold, detached, dry. He, himself, offers the explanation:

In the matter of style, I do not so describe that my subjective feelings can be detected in the sentences. In writing, I subdue to a dry, mathematical style what has come out of warm and profound feeling. But only such a style can be an awakener; for the reader must cause warmth and feeling to awaken in himself. He cannot simply allow these to flow into him from the one setting forth the truth, while the clarity of his own mind remains obscured.

And thus the personality of Rudolf Steiner remains

concealed behind his writing. He can, however, always be reached through the actual work one does. It is only through our own labour and struggle that we begin to recognize increasingly his labour for us.

What is that labour to which our own inner life has called us, other than to find our bearings in spiritual life, even as nature has placed us into physical life? With what infinite care and precision is the embryo carried from conception in the spirit to physical birth. Can the process leading to the second birth be any less caring and exact? 'The way to freedom is along the road of necessity'; let us follow this thought in the subsequent pages, and in its light, carry further what has been said, in a preliminary way in the second chapter, in regard to the basic books.

In *Initiation and its Results* [1] we are guided to work on what are called by an oriental name 'lotus flowers', astral or soul organs of perception. The first such organ to which we are directed is the sixteen-petalled lotus flower with eight exercises related to it. Eight of these petals belonging to times of natural or instinctive clairvoyance have grown dark with the human descent from spirit into matter. We stand at the zero point, and begin the ascent by developing the remaining eight petals to consciously acquired faculties of vision for the future. They are exercises above all in watchfulness over our habits of life.

Be watchful of your thoughts that they be truly meaningful.

Be watchful of your resolves that they be well-conceived and well-maintained.

Be watchful of your words, that they be neither too many nor too few, and learn to heed the words of others.

Be watchful of your outer undertakings that they be in

[1] Later published as the second half of *Knowledge of Higher Worlds* beginning with the chapter *Some Effects of Initiation*.

harmony, as far as possible, with the outer circumstances.

Be watchful over your own manner of life, that you are
neither too hasty nor too tardy.

Be watchful of the high goals you set yourself that
you neither undertake what is at present beyond your
capacities nor fall short of what is within them.

Be watchful in your readiness to learn from all that life
brings your way, even from a little child.

Be watchful that you maintain all the foregoing in right
accord with one another.

Here is a firm foundation for a beginning. Next we are
led to consider the twelve-petalled lotus flower with its
corresponding six exercises. These require greater effort
of concentration. They carry the work to a deeper level.
Whereas the previous exercises had more to do with
understanding-perception, these may be described as being
concerned with fostering greater heart-perception. They
again require the cultivation of certain faculties: control of
thought, control of action, inner tranquillity, positivity of
outlook, freedom from prejudice and pre-judgement, the
maintaining of the foregoing in a state of inner equilibrium.
So we move on from organ to organ, the demands
increasing with each step, but always supported by the
work done previously. Thus, through work, and answering grace, we advance as far as our destiny allows. It is clear
that such work, faithfully pursued, must lead to greater
health, balance and security in inner life, and to greater
ability to serve in outer life. The author recalls an experience
he once had of climbing Snowdon in Wales at night. There
were three in the party including the guide, an experienced
mountaineer who knew every inch of the way. We had to
follow his instructions step by step in total darkness as
he led the way round protruding ridge and narrow ledge,
always climbing until, with the first rays of dawn, we found

ourselves creeping along a great ridge with a steep drop below. So, by degrees, we arrived at the summit, to be rewarded with a magnificent sunrise. We realized then that, among the several approaches to that summit, we had followed the most dangerous. But he had never faltered, and we followed with perfect trust. Along a spiritual path we surely need no lesser guidance from one who has been before. Only here it is rocks and boulders, declivities, and obstacles in inner life we have to surmount or circumvent.

The study of the lotus flowers and the groups of exercises connected with each of them is clearly described in the book itself. Here we would wish to give an indication only of how the approach to exercises can take a different form from the one previously outlined. Each group of exercises has its own organic unity and function in relation to that particular lotus flower and the higher faculties to which it would ultimately lead. It will be seen how all the exercises are directed to developing stronger inner disciplines in the practice and achievement of moral forces and faculties, for only these can serve for a higher development.

Let us look again at the book *Theosophy*. The first chapter describes the various members composing the human being, those already acquired in long ages past, and those to be acquired in the course of further evolution. The ego stands as the active agent transmuting past into future.

It is one of the wonders of anthroposophical spiritual science that the greatest can find expression in the least, and vice versa. Thus, once we have grasped the nature of the threefold man, it enables us to recognize in him the seed potentials related to the very highest, even to the Holy Trinity. And, indeed, time and again, in order to understand the smallest we have to reach out to the greatest. This is quite particularly so in the study of man.

In *Theosophy* we are concerned primarily with what a man can make of himself in one life, of the consequences of this in the life after death, and how this, in turn, conditions his life in the following incarnation. We are guided from familiar considerations, to heights from which we can still survey the landscape, but then are led on into realms beyond our conscious experience, yet maintaining all the way a sense of reality on which we can fully rely. Thus we pass through soul regions and spirit regions, until we return to earth once again. How is this to be achieved without the reader, at some time, having to abandon his sense of freedom, falling back to mere credulity? To understand this is vital to our theme. Just here Rudolf Steiner describes his method of procedure in writing the book:

Let it be noted how . . . my Theosophy is developed. At every step taken in the book, spiritual perception stands in the background. Nothing is said which is not derived from spiritual perception; but, while the steps are being made, the perception is clothed at first, in the beginning of the book, in scientific ideas, until, in rising to higher realms, it must occupy itself more and more in fully picturing the spiritual world. But this picturing grows out of the natural-scientific as the blossom of a plant grows from the stem and leaves. As the plant is not seen in its entirety if it is considered only up to the blossom, so nature is not experienced in its entirety if we do not rise from the sensible to the super-sensible.

So what I strove for was to set out in anthroposophy the objective continuation of science, not to place by the side of science something subjective. It was inevitable that precisely this effort was not at first understood. Science was supposed to end with what antedates anthroposophy, and there was no inclination so to put life into the ideas of science as to lead to the comprehension of the spiritual. People were under the spell of the habit of thought developed during the second half of the nineteenth century. They could not muster the courage to break the fetters of mere sense-perception; they thought that they might arrive at regions where everybody asserts the validity of his own fantasy.

It has to be seen that this sense-bound thinking makes the spirit a slave to matter. It sets up the illusion that truth is to be found only by further analysis of matter. This kind of thinking has been infiltrated into the mind. It is so little born of the human spirit that it ends by negating that very spirit. Materialistic thinking is a darkening of the spirit not due to the phenomena men behold but to the way they behold them. The latter makes matter into the *all*, and the spirit into *nothing*. Only by overcoming this illusion inherent in materialistic thinking can the human spirit find its way out of darkness into light.

Rudolf Steiner's detached way of writing is further exemplified in his *Occult Science, an Outline*. In the opening chapter he reviews both the possible questionings of the scientist and the objections that might be raised by the religious minded. Their difficulties are taken seriously. In the second chapter there is again built up a picture of the members that make up a human being. The third chapter goes into a study of sleep and death, offering a further approach to the understanding of reincarnation. Sleep is described as a younger brother of death.

Anyone who does not continually draw strength for his weakened forces from sleep must of necessity destroy his life. Likewise, a world concept which is not fructified by a knowledge of the hidden world must lead to desolation. It is similar with death. Living beings succumb to death in order that new life may arise. It is only a knowledge of the supersensible which can shed clear light upon the beautiful words of Goethe: "Nature created death that she might have more abundant life."

The chapter leads us on a path through death to a new

life. Then follows a mighty chapter which is the heart of the book, *Man and the Evolution of the World*. This gives a vast panorama beginning with the dawn of world creation. It describes the successive stages in the creation of man together with all the ranks of hierarchies participating in this, see page 80 *et seq*. The chapter resounds like a mighty symphony for those prepared to hear it, yet it is written in a strictly formal manner.

We are led in successive cycles of time down to our own day. Chapter five is concerned with the modern path of initiation and the knowledge of man as a microcosm within the macrocosm. Then, the following chapter opens a view into future stages of human and world evolution. This book was published in 1908, only six years after the first issue of *Lucifer-Gnosis*. Now, all these decades later, we can recognize what an act of courage it was to put such a book on the open market.

With regard to the use of the book and the work involved in self-training, we quote the following:

> We need not think that it is necessary to pass through these stages successively, one after the other. On the contrary, the training may proceed in such a way, in accordance with the individuality of the student of spiritual science, he may have reached only a certain degree of perfection in a preceding stage when he begins exercises which correspond to a subsequent stage.
>
> . . . The way to knowledge of supersensible worlds described here is one which every human being can follow, no matter what the situation is in which he may find himself within the present day conditions of life. When describing such a path we must consider that the goal of knowledge and truth is the same in all ages of Earth evolution, but that the starting points of the human being on the path have been different in different ages. . . . The path to higher knowledge described here is eminently

fit for souls who incarnate in the immediate present. It is one which places the point of departure for spiritual development just where the human being now stands in any situation presented by modern life.

These last words are meant to be taken quite literally. The cultivation of anthroposophy does not require withdrawal to some lone retreat for peace and contemplation. On the contrary, one is asked to learn to create for oneself moments of quiet retreat whilst in the midst of everyday life.

It was during the time between the appearance of the *Philosophy of Freedom in* 1894 and his departure for Weimar in 1897 that Rudolf Steiner had two vital experiences which he refers to only briefly in *The Course of my Life.*

To him it was clear that a right science of nature must of itself lead to a science of the spirit. What was it that infiltrated materialistic thinking into the mind of man to prevent this? It was a kind of betrayal of the human spirit due to the working of certain beings of opposition. In the book of the Apocalypse it speaks of a battle between Michael and his angel host, and the Satanic hosts which were cast down to earth where they continue to molest man and could even destroy human civilization for all time. We quote the relevant sentence:

> In the thinking which can result from the science of nature — but which did not result at that time — I saw the basis upon which man might attain to insight into the world of spirit. I laid much stress, therefore, upon the knowledge which underlies nature, which must lead to the knowledge of the spirit.

Spiritually perceived there are beings for whom "it is absolute truth that the world must be a machine", any trend in thought that leads to such a conclusion is inspired by them.

Rudolf Steiner speaks of his "inner struggle against the demonic Powers who wanted to cause the knowledge of nature to become, not perception of spirit, but a mechanistic–materialistic way of thinking". Further: "*At that time I had to save my spiritual perception by inner battles. These battles were the background of my outer experience* [author's italics].

These beings, called by Rudolf Steiner Ahrimanic, can also be called spirits of darkness. It is they that have to be fought and overcome if humanity is to be led out of Kali-yuga into a new age of dawning spiritual light.

Here then is one part of the task that lay before Rudolf Steiner at that time. The other concerns our relationship to Christianity. He writes:

In this time of testing I succeeded in progressing further only when in spiritual vision I brought before my mind the evolution of Christianity.

The Christianity which I had to seek I did not find anywhere in the creeds. After the time of testing had subjected me to stern battles of the soul, I had to submerge myself in Christianity and, indeed, in the world in which the spiritual speaks thereof.

As regards his *Christianity as Mystical Fact* he writes: ". . . nothing existing in these documents have I inserted into the content unless I had first confronted this in the spirit." But then, what he wrote there opposed in many ways the customary doctrines. Out of these struggles, he could write:

The true substance of Christianity began germinally to unfold within me as an inner phenomenon of knowledge. About the turn of the century, the germ unfolded more and more. Before this turn of the century came the testing of the soul I have described. The unfolding of my soul rested upon the fact that *I had stood in spirit before the*

Mystery of Golgotha in most inward, most earnest solemnity of knowledge [author's italics].

Here was the other half of his initiate task in leading out of Kali-yuga into a new future.

It is expected that the age following Kali-yuga, in which a new consciousness is to awaken in humanity, will last 2,500 years. It is revealed in anthroposophy that the age predicted in the Gospel as that of Christ's second coming belongs to the same era – that within the next 2,500 years, humanity as a whole will experience the Christ, not in the flesh, but even as Paul experienced him at Damascus. Paul had said of himself that he had come before his time. That time has arrived. This is the innermost secret and the great reality of this Age of Light in which we all live. Anthroposophy has come to prepare mankind for this. To behold the Christ in his second coming, man has to raise himself to etheric vision. That is the interpretation which anthroposophy gives to the Gospel image of Christ's coming 'upon the clouds'. We stand at the very beginning of an apocalyptic time and have inwardly to prepare to meet it, each one according to his destiny.

Meaning in History

The Question

WHERE SHALL we seek for meaning in history? That is the question we have to explore.

In today's terms we live with a big bang theory at the beginning, and a heat death theory at the end. What meaning can this offer to human history or to existence at all? Yet, this is all that science has arrived at. The fact that man has come to have a consciousness that asks the question remains an insoluble enigma.

Have the humanities more to tell us? They bring us a wide range of experiences, joys and sorrows, laughter and tears, triumphs and defeats both in inner and outer life, but all are transitory without a hint of any ultimate direction or goal. Yes, there are men of vision, Shakespeare with his *Tempest*, Goethe with his *Faust*, Shelley with his *Prometheus Unbound*; we rejoice to have their gifts but in the end, what more do they tell us than that "We are such stuff as dreams are made on". If we abide by the scientific view that is all they can possibly tell us.

Otto Spengler's *Decline of the West* woke attention early in the century. His thesis is that a cultural period consists of a youthful era of growth and creativity, but when this reaches its peak, then comes civilization and decline. He compares our present state with the decline of Rome. As for the future, there is only the surmise that another dominant culture may arise as appears to have been the case in the past. Egypt, Greece, the Middle Ages each has its distinctive character but there is nothing to suggest continuity from the one to the other. His descriptions are of passing

78

phenomena. Of further meaning there is no trace.

The author once asked a group of children aged twelve whom he had been telling about the life of St. Francis, what they thought was the difference between a legend and history. The reply came: "The legend is more true because it tells you what history can't." How right they were!

How was it in earlier times, before the age of modern science when religious faith was still strong? Then human life found its meaning in ultimate union with God. The spiritual worlds were felt to be close at hand. Legends, visions, dreams, were convincing and plentiful. We think of Joan of Arc. An untutored country girl made her way to the court of the Dauphin to tell that she had heard the voice of the archangel Michael. She was to drive the English out of France and make the Dauphin King. What concerns us here is that she was believed. She actually did lead the French to victory and forced the English to retire. The possibility of spiritual intervention through such a maid was accepted – life on earth was still felt to be guided from above. Her earthly reward was to be burnt at the stake as a witch. She held to her story to the end, a story that has fired the imagination as few have. That she heard a voice has to be credited her else there would be no story. But how many really accept the voice as a call from the archangel Michael? Joan's intervention changed the history of Europe, of France and England in particular. But that there could be such direct spiritual guidance in human affairs is something lost to our time though it was felt to be natural only a few hundred years ago. Human history was felt to be part of a great cosmic plan. Rudolf Steiner reveals that it was indeed the archangel Michael who directed Joan and that her faith was founded on reality.

As we go further back in time, legend, vision, dream, play an ever greater part. As a further instance of this we quote the remarkable circumstances of the founding of the official Christian Church. Constantine in the fourth

79

century AD experienced what the books describe as a 'conspicuous miracle'. On the eve of a battle with a far greater force than his own, he had a vision of a flaming cross in the sky at noon with the words 'By this conquer'. He won the battle. Later, as Emperor Constantine, in 324 AD he declared Christianity to be the official religion of the empire.

There is another significant circumstance belonging to this time. Christmas had always been celebrated on the sixth of January to commemorate the descent of Christ into Jesus at the baptism. As generation followed generation the understanding of the baptism began to wane and with it the distinction between the man Jesus and the divinity of Christ.

The early Church Fathers regarded the birth of Jesus as a birth in the flesh, and the event of the baptism as a birth in the spirit. It was in Constantine's time, or shortly after, that the child birth became the traditional Christmas, and the Epiphany receded into the background. Just at the point where the outer church became firmly grounded and the persecution of the Christians was brought to a halt, the inner and greater mystery of the Christ birth grew more obscure. This kind of situation repeats continuously – an advance towards outer life and a corresponding dimming in inner life.

We ask, when was history as we know it, that is, as a recording of outer events, first born? It leads back to Herodotus, the acclaimed father of history. He lived in the fifth century BC. It is astonishing to think that history as we know it is only two thousand five hundred years old. The world of myth and legend was still abundantly rich in the Greek soul, though in a lessening degree. Herodotus, a great traveller, wrote out of his own varied life experience. He was a type of modern man in his day. Thus history from its beginning is concerned with the temporary rather than the eternal.

We have already referred to the fact that writing goes back no further than to Egypt, about 3,300 B C. Those early inscriptions on monuments and temple walls tell of the dynasties, the customs of the people, but all is pervaded still with a sense of the spiritual mysteries behind outer life. Rudolf Steiner tells us that the first writing was born as direct vision of the spiritual was dying out. It is interesting to note that it was just then that Kali-yuga began. Divorced from the spirit, history becomes an empty vessel. Without the spirit what real meaning can history have? Spiritual Science came to meet us just when Kali-yuga ended. A new light is to be kindled for the understanding of life and destiny on this earth.

To begin with man confronts a double dilemma. Looking outwards he is persuaded by science to identify himself with matter, and looking inwards, to merge his being with the animal world of instincts. Either way he is lost to himself.

Thus Rudolf Steiner faced a double task; on the one hand to free science from materialism, on the other to reveal to man his true source of being. Science has sought for the infinitesimal particle from which to build up its notion of the world. Spiritual science or anthroposophy, on the contrary, takes its start from the universal realm of divine being and descends, stage by stage, in the story of creation.

Christ, walking as man on earth, said to his disciples: "I am the Alpha and the Omega", the beginning and the end. In so far as it is given to man also to be able to say 'I am', what part has he in that statement of Christ? His words tell us we are in a transition stage between a coming into being and a passing away. He said: "I am with you always even unto the end of the world", and he also said, "heaven and earth will pass away but my word will not pass away." What part has man in the living word? How has man arrived at what he is? What is his responsible rôle in the present? What opens up for him as future?

Cosmic Background

Turning once again to chapter four in *Occult Science, an Outline*, we are asked to make a prodigious leap in imagination to unheard of states of being. If we are prepared to take this leap in thought and imagination, there opens up an immense saga of events following on one another, including all the hierarchical beings of antiquity, still known to Aristotle and to early Christianity. Stage by stage we learn to see how the history of man and his world are invested with profoundest meaning, how the present state of man and the world become ever more understandable, and what real tasks and challenges meet us for the future. A view opens up that calls on us to proceed step by step, not only as earthly beings possessed of mind and conscience, but as spiritual and immortal natures having an assigned rôle to play in regard to the great goals of human and world evolution. We learn that in the whole history of the world from the dawn of creation to the present moment nothing is unrelated. So, too, we learn to see the world of nature around us including man as one integral whole in which no single feature stands alone. Only in so far as the world grows to a unity of past, present, and future, can human life gather meaning and purpose. The law of each for all and all for each becomes abundantly clear, not as a law imposed from without, as was the case when humanity was still in its childhood, but as the law of one's innermost being ever since Christ, moving amongst men, said, "I am come to fulfil the law". What was once conformity to outer law has now become a path of inner fulfilment.

We have been partly prepared for this journey through chapter four in the preceding pages in our consideration of the four elements, fire, air, water, earth. We have seen how these are related to man in his fourfold constitution of Ego, astral body, etheric body, and physical body, and how through the elements of air, water and earth, the kingdoms of animal, plant and mineral are gathered around him. Now, looking to the body of the earth as a whole, that, too, consists of the four elements: an independent zone of warmth, the thermosphere; the atmosphere; the hydrosphere including the mists and vapours; and lastly the lithosphere, the mineral rock. We are accustomed to see these as separate zones. It is possible, however, to consider the earth as an organic whole: a physical body by virtue of the rocks; an encircling life through the plants; possessing a sentient life through the animals; and finally the consciousness of man as being also part of her being. There was a time when the earth was felt to be a mother, when men would prostrate themselves out of love for Mother Earth. The earth and its kingdoms are one. The earth in its wholeness embodies form, life, soul, and consciousness. Perceived in this way, the planet earth becomes a being in its own right, a heavenly body, maintained by an 'intelligence' uniquely its own. Even in the late Middle Ages one spoke of the *intelligences* of the heavenly bodies and the harmony of the spheres.

Truly we need to learn to love the Earth; the steadfast strength of its rocks, the flowing rhythmic life of its plants, the joy of motion of its animals, the contemplative depth of human awareness, the earth as habitat of all this vast variety with its resplendent and manifold beauties. The astronauts, beholding it from outside, were filled with wonder at its beauty as a heavenly body, their planetary home. Beyond all that, is the mystery of its movement around its own axis, making day and night, and its orbital flight bringing the wondrous round of the seasons. There may begin to awaken in us subtler feelings and impressions such as the sages had of old, in seeing the earth in all its manifestations as the handiwork of a world of divine beings. We, today, have to struggle to rid ourselves of the spectre of the earth as a spinning top of inert matter carrying an accidental life upon its surface.

In the spiritual worlds there are beings, relationships

between beings, and activities arising through these relationships. What we regard as outer objects in nature are manifestations of such hidden workings. Where today's science speaks of masses and energies, spiritual science speaks of the will and substance of beings. There is no outer nature unrelated to beings. Asked whether the heavenly beings have ideals comparable to the ideals of human beings, Rudolf Steiner replied that their ideal is man, man in his becoming. In so far as they participate in man's becoming, they carry their own evolution forward. Thus they have their own destinies and yet form an integral part of human destiny.

For man nothing is more intimate and exalted than to discover that as a threefold being he is directly related to the Holy Trinity, to the will of the Father, the love of the Son, the light of the Holy Spirit. The hierarchical beings have been known in the mystery schools from all time. They make the three-times three choirs of angels. The following are their names:

	Greek	Christian	Spiritual Science
Beings of	Seraphim	Seraphim	Seraphim
the first	Cherubim	Cherubim	Cherubim
hierarchy	Thrones	Thrones	Spirits of Will
Beings of	Kyriotetes	Dominions	Spirits of Wisdom
the second	Dynamis	Mights	Spirits of Movement
hierarchy	Exusiai	Powers	Spirits of Form
Beings of	Archai	Principalities	Spirits of Personality
the third	Archangeloi	Archangels	Archangels
hierarchy	Angeloi	Angels	Angels

Beyond these beings in their ascending glories is the Trinity they serve.

We may now, in briefest outline, give the main guide lines in chapter four of *Occult Science, an Outline*.

The earth as we know it passed through three previous conditions or, more accurately, through three earlier planetary incarnations, to arrive at its present state.

The first of these came about through the deeds of sacrifice of exalted beings named Thrones or Spirits of Will. They, having reached fulfilment in their own evolution at the stage they had then reached, gave freely of their own substance to provide the ground for another, a new evolution, that of man. The substance thus offered was outer physical warmth born of an inner gift of love. This constituted the first beginning of an outer world creation. Within the manifold streams of warmth, as described, there were laid down the germinal seeds of what, after aeons of time, were to become the physical bodies of today.

There can be no greater contrast than this description of an all-encompassing world of warmth at the beginning as sacrificial deed and the modern physicist's view of a universal spiritless heat death at the end.

It is typical of anthroposophy to find connections between what is nearest and what seems most remote. For instance, the intimate relationship between will and warmth is immediately familiar: every exercise of energy or will releases its measure of warmth. But further than that, upon the warmth man bears within him, his blood warmth, depends his balance of health and his very life, yet how that warmth is generated and how maintained, and how physical warmth relates to moral warmth are questions that remain far from common explanation. It is also a remarkable fact that our body warmth of 98.4°F is well above the temperature of our rooms, normally set for comfort at 68-70°F; we thus carry a warmth body of our own distinct from the environment. It is thus not altogether difficult to conceive of a lifeline from the warmth in man to the warmth at the dawn of creation.

Greek mythology speaks of that age as the age of Chronos. Out of timelessness was born time which set the course for human evolution until its culmination when time will again cease to be. Beyond the physical germs, as regards life, soul and spirit, the human being rested in the divine. At the end of this great cosmic age, all that was thus far created was drawn back into a state of purely spiritual existence called *Pralaya* – a state bearing comparison with man's passage through the spiritual worlds between successive incarnations.

Then all re-emerged at a more advanced stage, and into the work of outer creation there now streamed the sacrificial deeds and substance of the Kyriotetes, the Dominions or Spirits of Wisdom. The first creation was one of outer darkness. Now there was born the world of Light and with it the creation of Space. As one can speak of inner and outer warmth, so, too, of inner and outer light, inner and outer space, the one aspect more inward and spiritual, the other more outward and physical. As the Light radiated through the previously created Warmth, the latter underwent a partial condensation into Air, not yet air as we know it, yet giving rise to a kind of pulsation, mirroring life. The physical germs were thus endowed with a quality of life. The air can be regarded as the shadow aspect of the Light, a difficult conception as things are viewed today.

In these descriptions we must imagine that we are dealing with measureless aeons of time, with cosmic dimensions. There came a second Pralaya followed by the third stage of .creation. To the deeds of the Spirits of Will and the Spirits of Wisdom, were added the gifts and the workings of the Spirits of Movement. Into creation there entered the world of Tone, Harmony, changeful relationships through Movement. This finds reflection in our world of music, but also in all matters of ratio and proportion that rule in substance, in the secret workings of chemistry, for example. Thus in a higher sphere, beyond Warmth there is engendered Light, and beyond Light Tone, so below, warmth condenses into air and air further into the fluid nature of water – the water that lives in colour, chemistry and life. Substance had arrived at an organic consistency resembling horn but had not yet mineralized further. Corresponding to the three elements, warmth, air and water, Rudolf Steiner describes three intermediary kingdoms, mineral-plant, plant-animal, and animal-man. Man in his spiritual being had not yet finally descended but, still from divine heights shone down upon the physical, etheric and astral natures below. There were now sentient forms possessed of elementary nerve, sense, respiratory, circulatory and digestive organs.

And now, this vast complexity of life and being withdrew into a further Pralaya to emerge finally, stage by stage, as our present planet Earth. It was the Exusiai, the Spirits of Form, the Elohim of the Old Testament, who now let their powers stream into the world in its further shaping, reaching through warmth, air and water to the mineral rocks, the fourth element, earth. This rock is the floor of the world on which man was finally to descend to pursue his destiny in growing awareness of his own identity. Here on earth he is to establish ultimately out of his own waking consciousness and directed will, his relationship with the hierarchies of his begetting.

Out of earlier sources, Rudolf Steiner named the previous planetary incarnations, Ancient Saturn, Ancient Sun and Ancient Moon, not to be confused with the bodies bearing the same names in our solar system.

The Present Earth

When the earth emerged from Pralaya it had to recapitulate the earlier conditions to reach its present stage. Spiritual Science tells of a Polarian age of warmth, a Hyperborean age of warmth and air, a Lemurian age of warmth, air and water; and then how in Atlantean times the fourth element came into being making the final condition of warmth, air, water and earth as described earlier. It was only then, with the deposition of the solid mineral substance that the human being could finally assume his vertical shape though this had been partly prepared for in late Lemuria. The composition of the human body was still plastic and largely fluidic and could therefore dissolve away without leaving any trace in the rocks. That is why geology has failed to find any fossil form that could have been the direct ancestor of present man. Rather the reverse is the case, the primitive fossil types represent a premature descent and fixation into densifying matter. In this we may recognize the law of restraint ruling in human development to which reference has already been made. The human form was ideally present from the beginning but was the last to reach full outer manifestation. We may imagine this ideal form very slowly descending into substance and answering ascending forms being arrested whilst the central stream carrying humanity forward could continue to evolve further. Le Comte de Noüy in his *Human Destiny* goes so far as to describe the animal kingdom as the debris of human development.

It follows that the existing rocks of the earth, though they, too, form a sequence in line with that of the great earth stages, must all have appeared only in the course of Atlantean times. Rudolf Steiner describes them as merely reflecting at a much later time what had gone before. This is shown in the following table.

WITHIN ATLANTEAN TIMES

The Azoic Age	As yet no fossils	a reflection of Polaria
The Palaeozoic Age	showing early life forms up to fishes and coal flora	a reflection of Hyperborea
The Mesozoic Age	with a great increase in fossil types up to reptiles	a reflection of Lemuria
The Kainozoic Age	with more recent and advanced fossils up to mammals and modern flora	reflection of Atlantis itself

The most recent rocks of all since the last glacial age, 10,000 BC are described as containing "The Age of Man".

This indicates how man as we know him was the *last* to descend to the earth though the first to be conceived at the very dawn of creation.

In imagination we may look back to a time when Adam and Eve as human prototypes were now created. In consciousness they still were in a paradisal state of innocence surrounded by ethereal glory. Then came the event of the Temptation and Fall in late Lemuria. This brought a rude awakening through Lucifer out of a state of blissful innocence to find themselves now stripped bare – 'naked and ashamed'. At the same time their consciousness was darkened towards the heavens and God so that they felt 'cast out' of Paradise into a world of labour and of pain. This proclaimed the birth of earthly human history. Yet man stepped into this history uniquely as an upright being. By mid-Atlantis he had acquired the utterance of linguistic sounds as distinct from the nature cries of other creatures. By the end of Atlantis he could experience the first beginnings of thought and a premonitory sense of self. What the child of today achieves in the first three years of life, it took humanity many thousands of years to reach. Rudolf Steiner gives a vivid description of this in his book *Atlantis and Lemuria* also published under the title of *Cosmic Memory*. All through this time the spiritual guidance of mankind was maintained through Mystery Schools, conducted at first by divine beings, and later, in course of time, by the most advanced and loftiest members of the human race.

The destruction of the continent of Atlantis and its eventual sinking beneath what is now the Atlantic Ocean gave rise to a period of great migrations eastward across Europe and North Africa to Asia, but also westward as can be seen in common features of origin in ancient Peking and Peru. The transition from Atlantean to post-Atlantean times is evidenced in part by legends of the great flood that followed the ice age of ten thousand years ago. Such a legend is the Old Testament story of Noah and the ark. "And the waters prevailed exceedingly, and all the high hills that were under the whole heaven were covered. Fifteen cubits upward did the waters prevail; and the mountains were covered . . . And after the end of the hundred and fifty days the waters were abated . . . and the ark rested upon the mountains of Ararat".

After forty days Noah sent forth a dove and it returned by evening. He sent it forth a second time and this time it returned with an olive leaf in its beak. Then he sent it out again, always with seven days between, but this time it did not return. This was the sign that it was time to leave the ark. There, on the newly uncovered land, "Noah builded an altar unto the Lord . . . and offered burnt offerings on the altar". And then came something quite new. "And God spoke unto Noah and to his sons . . . I establish my covenant with you and with your sons after you". What was this covenant? "I do set my bow in the cloud, and it shall be a token between me and the earth". The token was the first rainbow.

We can imagine that Atlantis was always under mist and the minds of the humans also. With the rainbow a new light dawned in the heavens and for the earth, and in the human mind. The Lord even added, "and it shall come to pass, when I bring a cloud over the earth, that the bow shall be seen in the cloud: and I will remember my covenant which is between me and you . . ." This was the beginning of a new relationship between man and God as the point of departure for a new era. The whole of post-Atlantean culture has to do with successive stages in the awakening of man, to his own selfhood, his egohood, his growing to be one with his God, the God of the I AM.

The Culture Epochs in Natural Progression

Otto Spengler in his book, *Decline of the West,* written earlier in the century compares our time with that of the decline of Rome. He describes three successive cultures; Ancient Egypt, Greece and the Middle Ages. He shows how each rises to its peak and passes into decline; the creative wealth of Greece into the prosaic life of Rome, the beauty of the Middle Ages into the mechanistic times we live in.

There is no visible connection between them, nor do they leave anything behind on which to build further. What is to follow, whether there will arise another such dominant culture, is left to chance and mere surmise.

Anthroposophy takes the view that no culture can arise except if it be born of man. Changes of culture imply changes in man. It is to man, therefore, we must look if we seek for answers. He, alone, is the connecting link from the one to the other.

What we see first and foremost in viewing a Greek temple are the rising columns uniting, as it were, a world above with the earth below. Very different is the impression of a Gothic cathedral with its great arches lifting heavenwards as though to take with them the prayers of the people below. Different again is the lofty dome of St. Peter, designed by Michaelangelo, coming later as though to assemble the thoughts for the new age begun.

Looked at in the light of man, we may see in the above progression a law deeply inherent and operative in human nature, the passage from limb to heart to head.

This sequence we have met already in our consideration of childhood progress up to the age of three and may come to see in this a recapitulation of the three outstanding achievements, by divine intervention over long ages of time, on the vanished and forgotten continent of Atlantis: the raising of man to the upright walk, the articulated word, the lighting up of thought – the three hallmarks of man's being for all times to come.

Rudolf Steiner speaks of these three interventions as the three pre-Golgotha deeds of Christ, the God who named himself, I am. These were the preparatory stages for a time, still in the far future, when the being of man would be able to pronounce from within himself the words *I am*, and this for all mankind without exception.

This teaches us that man, even from the beginning, was never an animal as this word is understood today. The ani-

mals fall into species, each species carrying its distinguish-
ing features. Humanity, despite all the groups and communities into which it is divided, is of one single species.
Hence the words of Paul hold good of all the peoples, many
members but one body; moreover imbued with one spirit,
for all human beings, no matter what the language, are united in their pronouncing of the words *I am*. To arrive at
this, all are led through the sequence of the three periods of
childhood up to the coming of age at twenty-one, the birth
of the ego and entrance into adult life.

This same sequence may be followed on the greatest possible scale in the succession of the culture epochs. Following
Atlantis which, as we have noted, provided man with his
basic physical framework, we come to the first of the named
culture epochs, the Ancient Indian. We have to realise that
this epoch belongs to legendary times. What we know of it,
though confirmed by spiritual science, comes down to us
by oral tradition, recorded millenia later when a script became available for the first time.

The outstanding feature of this epoch, still preserved in
Hindu tradition, is the caste system, established by the
Seven Holy Rishis of long, long ago, who drew their inspiration and authority for this from the highest spiritual
sources. The caste system was a social structure built on the
interworking of the four primeval elements in nature: fire,
air, water and earth, represented socially by priest, ruler,
merchant or artisan and worker (Brahmin, Kshatrya,
Vasya, Sudra). These are the four forces that build the formative life of the etheric body. Thus was the physical entity
derived from Atlantis endowed with an etheric body.
Steiner tells us that the sacred Vedas we have today are but
an echo of the glory of the original; so far back is the caste
system.

The second culture epoch, the Ancient Persian, though
coming two thousand years later, still belongs to the legendary. This was under the guidance of the exalted Priest-

King, Zarathustra (Zoro Aster, Golden Star). He drew his wisdom from the Sun-spirit Ahara Mazdao whom he foresaw, even then, as descending one day to mankind on earth. His task was to awaken his people to the great drama of the battle of the gods of Light and Darkness(Ormuzd and Ariman). Thus he was able to implant a soul life, as astral body, into the already existing physical and etheric bodies. Of this great culture, as Steiner described it, there are a few lingering echoes but nothing extant to show it ever existed.

It is along these stages, Atlantis, Ancient India, Ancient Persia, that we arrive at the first outwardly manifested culture and civilisation, the Ancient Egyptian. Humanity, now possessed of the three basic bodies or sheaths, physical, etheric and astral, can be said to have reached, at an all-human level, the equivalent of the coming-of-age of the human being of today and is therefore ready, for the first time, to receive the incoming ego. From this point it becomes possible to draw a close analogy between the first stages of adult life, beginning at 21, and the culture of Ancient Egypt, and the further progression of the culture epochs.

Thus, in the first period of adult life, 21 to 28, the young person is mainly concerned with taking hold of his own life and finding his bearings in life as a whole. The task of the ego is to lift and transform what is instinctive and uncon-.scious to the level of conscious and responsible participation. Expressed in spiritual terms, in this 21 to 28 year period, the ego is working mainly on the astral body to arrive at a more conscious inner life of soul, named sentient-soul.

Correspondingly, Ancient Egypt steps out of pre-history to become the first fully expressed outer culture and civilisation, the first to leave behind a heritage of monuments and created works, the first to arrive at a written script and recorded history. It is the first culture to build an outer social life embodying religion, art and, in its own degree, a

93

science of the stars, medicine, agriculture, trade. In the Pharoah there stands before us the figure of a representative ego-bearer for the whole people. The Egyptian epoch may be regarded as ego-directed at the level of the sentient-soul.

At the second stage of adult life, 28 to 35, one should arrive at greater self-mastery, and be more responsible in intercourse with others both in the sharing and exchanging of ideas and in mutual undertakings with and for one another. The ego, during this time, is working on the formative life of the etheric body, developing thereby mind-, rational- or intellectual-soul.

Correspondingly, it is in the fourth, the Graeco-Roman culture epoch, that in Greece there is born philosophy, the art of reason (superbly demonstrated in the Socratic dialogues), the art of rhetoric and the birth of drama and, indeed, an advance to a high degree of all the arts. In Rome, in this same epoch, there is born the status of the citizen and citizen rights.

This epoch can be described particularly as that of the mind-soul.

We are now living in the Fifth Post-Atlantean culture epoch. This is still very young, having begun only in the fifteenth century, and therefore with fifteen hundred years yet to go. We can therefore only refer to its dominant features up to the present. The ego, in this epoch, is working deepest on the physical body in which man fully finds himself. This has led to a highly accentuated sense of the self, and with this, an intense impulse to explore and to know the given environment, hence the term, the age of the consciousness-soul. This so far has been in terms of the material-physical and has led to a blinding of man to his own deeper-lying nature, as also in his relationship to the world. There are, today, gathering signs of impulses to transcend this self-boundedness in a matter-bound universe, and to carry the scientific impulse which has marked this age to a rediscovery of the spirit in man and in nature. Hence to the term consciousness-soul is added spiritual-soul. To aid towards this transition is the particular aim of anthroposophy or modern spiritual science and thus, also, to overcome the abyss between self and world, and between oneself and one's fellow human beings.

This epoch is under the zodiacal sign of Pisces. The following one, Aquarius, is looked to as the age of Philadelphia, the age of universal brotherhood. Beyond that again is the age of Capricorn, by a strange paradox the age prophesied to be the war of each against all. It perhaps might be conceived as a moral-spiritual battle on behalf of and not merely against one another.

To conclude, the three soul states – sentient-soul, rational- or mind-soul, and consciousness- or spiritual-soul – lead on according to spiritual science to three spiritual states; spirit-self, life-spirit, and spirit-man, known of old as Manas, Buddhi, and Atman.

Thus history runs its course both within man and through man, neither by chance nor merely pre-determined but as a striving evolutionary process. We move from man as the child of history to history as the creation of man.

The Post-Atlantean Cultural Epochs

The table that follows shows our modern epoch as having begun in AD 1413 and the preceding one, the Graeco-Roman, in 747 BC, an interval of 2160 years between the one and the other. Further, the modern age comes under the sign of Fishes, the previous one under the sign of the Ram. A similar span of time is allotted to each of the earlier epochs, each under its own constellation, for Ancient Egypt, the Bull, for Ancient Persia, the Heavenly Twins, Castor and Pollux, for Ancient India, Cancer. Going further back we reach with Leo into the final phase of Atlantis. If we follow the round of the zodiac through all twelve constellations this covers an era of twelve times 2160 or 25,920 years, a Platonic Year.

What underlies this is the fact that the solar and the stellar day are not identical. The sun always falls back a little. Since the year is reckoned from sunrise at the Spring equinox, the direction of the sun in relation to the Zodiac shifts a little each year by what is known as the equinoctial precession. It means that the sun moves from one constellation to the next, in this way it makes a complete round of the Zodiac in the course of a Platonic year.

In earlier times, right up to the end of the Middle Ages, the sun, moon, planets, and stars were felt to be one great cosmic community with man as a microcosmos within this macrocosmos. The sun was regarded as the Regent of the heavens, the spiritual as well as the physical source of light and life. Its position in relation both to the heavens and the earth was then one of paramount importance – a past wisdom which is lost to modern man.

The historical culture epochs as shown do not tally with the astronomical epochs which always fall earlier by as much as two or three centuries and vary in length according to the sizes of the constellations. These astronomical figures, accurate as outer measurements, show no discernible connection with the dates for the culture epochs which we are following in our historical survey.

The historical culture epochs as described by Rudolf Steiner follow an inner path. The hope is in connection with all genuine scientific exploration that these two modes of perceiving the world, may one day meet to confirm and fructify each other.

That is certainly the aim and direction of spiritual science, that spirit and matter, inner and outer, will one day be perceived each as a revelation of the other.

It will be obvious that there must be much overlapping of the epochs – nothing begins and ends abruptly, but the table below can serve as a broad guide. If we go further back by the same kind of reckoning, we arrive at the sign of the

Lion, Leo, in Atlantis.

Epoch	Dates	Zodiacal Sign	
Modern epoch	AD1413– AD3573	Fishes	Pisces
Graeco-Roman epoch	747BC– AD1413	Ram	Aries
Ancient Egyptian epoch	2907BC– 747BC	Bull	Taurus
Ancient Persian epoch	5067BC– 2907BC	Twins	Gemini
Ancient Indian epoch	7227BC– 5067BC	Crab	Cancer

We recall how, towards the end of Atlantis humanity was still in its early infancy. Another way of expressing it might be to say that humanity was still closely wrapped in the spiritualities, which means also that the very highest alone, the gods themselves and later the greatest of human initiates could provide the education and culture of the people of that time.

We cannot in this series include Chinese culture amongst the post-Atlantean cultures because in its spiritual origin it leads back to those high sources which pervaded Atlantis itself. Even the language formation is totally different from the Sanskrit of Ancient India, from which have descended most of our western languages with their cultures.

Anthroposophy describes how in Atlantis there were mystery schools or oracles guided by the intelligences of the planetary spheres. Greatest of these was the Sun-oracle, ruled and guided by the being we call today the archangel Michael. When the migrations began, the great initiate of the Sun-oracle led a company of his closest disciples eastward to a region in western Asia. From that supersensible spiritual centre were sent out impulses for the founding of the successive culture epochs as shown in the preceding table.

Ancient India

The culture of Ancient India was guided by the Seven Holy Rishis. Rudolf Steiner describes them as simple persons in daily life, but when they were together at certain times, they were totally transfigured. They were lifted up to the most exalted heights whence they brought back the wisdom needed to guide the people. The present *Rig-veda*, with all the sacred quality of its verses, gives but the faintest echo of their sublime teachings.

Another source of guidance for the Indian people was that of the beloved Krishna whose legendary life is celebrated in song and dance each year. He descends in times of great spiritual need as an Avatar, a messenger of the god, Vishnu. It is thus we meet him in the Bhagavadgita, the Song of Songs, as charioteer to the hero Arjun. There is to be a battle between kith and kin, a dreadful thing to contemplate since the blood bond was held to be the most sacred of all. Arjun shrinks back from this ordeal. Krishna teaches Arjun of reincarnation, that death to the body is not death to the soul, and that when a higher destiny calls we have to obey. In this teaching we may recognize the beginning of what is much later to meet us in the teachings of Christ leading out of community based on natural inheritance and the blood to community in the spirit.

An outstanding feature of Indian life is the perpetuation of the ancient caste system which nevertheless is wholly bound to the blood and the circumstances of birth. There the only consoling factor is the teaching of repeated earth lives. Buddha abolished caste in his teaching in the sixth century BC but it still rules in Hindu India. Mahatma Gandhi, who strove so nobly to retrieve the situation of the Pariahs, calling them the Children of God, himself remained a faithful Hindu.

We meet in the caste system in a spiritual cultural form the reality of the four elements descending from fire, to air, to water, to earth. At all times 'fire' is the holiest element, the element of highest love, devotion and sacrifice. So it is that the highest caste is that of the Brahmins, the priestly teachers who alone have access to the secret doctrine. Next below them are the Kshatriyas, the caste of the warriors, princes, rulers. They are taught out of the sacred books by the Brahmins, how to rule their dominions, the spaces they command, out of the will of the gods. Below the Kshatriyas are the Vaisyas, described as merchants, sometimes as artisans. They are the voyagers through the realms, carrying the necessities of life from one region to another – they represent the circulating waters that sustain the daily life. Last and humblest of all are the Sudras, most bound to the earth, yet each caste has its virtue and its ideal, and their particular virtue is patience, endurance, and trust in the high ruling of destiny.

The great longing in this first post-Atlantean culture was to reach back to the divine, the memory of which still lived on powerfully in souls. Therefore the world of outer nature is still felt to be strange, giving no sense of home, hence the term *maya*, usually translated as illusion. The illusion lay in imagining that there could be anything of abiding value in this transitory earth existence.

Sanskrit, as said earlier, is the mother source of most of our western languages. A highly cultured Indian, a scientist, once asked the author: "Why is it that when I read a line of Sanskrit I feel as though transported into a state of ecstasy, whilst the finest English poetry does not move me that way." The fact is as described by Rudolf Steiner that in the ancient languages the very sounds of the words quicken a sense of divine presence which is no longer possible to later language. The fact that Sanskrit is the mother source for the subsequent cultures makes an immediate bond between them so that they succeed one another, different though they are, somewhat like the succeeding phases in a human lifetime.

Ancient Persia

We pass on to take a similar glance at Ancient Persian culture. Unlike India, here spiritual guidance rests with one great individuality, Zarathustra, or Zoroaster, the golden Star. Rudolf Steiner has much to tell about him though there seems little or no evidence that he ever existed. Yet there are many notable legends about him.

One legend tells that Zarathustra dwelt in a cave high up a mountain from which he daily gazed into the Sun. There he beheld the Ahura Mazdao, the great Aura, the Sun within the sun, radiating light and life through all the world. A further legend tells that there was once revealed to him a vision of this Being, later named the Christ, enthroned with Eagle, Lion, Bull and a Human Form around him. He had the foreknowledge that that Being would once descend to earth.

The direction Zarathustra gave to culture was the very opposite of that of Ancient India. He taught love for the Earth. He drew down from the stars the calendar whereby to guide life according to the seasons. He introduced irrigation and agriculture. He taught that one of the most sacred places on earth was where the animal gave its droppings to the soil. He transformed the wolf into the faithful dog. Home and family were holy.

Zarathustra portrayed life as a great battle between Ahura Mazdao or Ormuzd, the god of light, and Ahriman, the god of darkness, a battle that, at that time, was fought by higher powers around the being of man who was still a child-man. Whereas the Indian teaching led the soul up to the heights, the teaching of Zarathustra was to lead the soul down so that man might learn to know himself a true denizen of the earth.

The *Zend Avesta* which, like the *Rig-veda*, was written down a long time later, contains a characteristic verse, a prayer to the beings who inspire good thoughts, good words, good deeds for protection against the beings who inspire evil thoughts, evil words, evil deeds.

Ancient Egypt

The Egyptian epoch comes far more within the scope of accessible knowledge. Rudolf Steiner revealed that Zarathustra had two intimate pupils to whom he imparted very special gifts out of his own nature. The one was Thoth-Hermes, the founder of Egyptian culture, the other Moses, the law-giver. The former could teach out of the wisdom of the stars; the latter out of the mysteries of time. Both, in their very different ways, were preparing for the coming of One who would say "I am come to fulfil the law". In both of these cultures, the soul-spiritual nature of man had entered more deeply into bodily incarnation, so that human life and human relationships acquired more of an individual character.

The ruling myth in Egyptian culture is that of the Sun-god Osiris. It tells that he descended to the earth, the abode of men, to help and guide them. He there incurred the enmity of his dark brother Typhon (Seth) who had other plans. Typhon brought about the death of Osiris and dismembered the body into fourteen parts which he buried separately in different places. Isis, the faithful consort of Osiris, came in search of him. She wandered through the whole land and for each part, as she found it, had a temple erected bearing his image.

Meanwhile the immortal Osiris re-ascended to heaven where he became the judge of the dead. As each soul, bearing her own Osiris within her, approached the great Osiris on his Judgment Seat, it was weighed in a balance by Thoth (Hermes). Then Osiris pronounced judgment for the life to come.

This powerful picture from the *Book of the Dead*, penetrated deep into Egyptian life. It foreshadowed how One would come and suffer death in the flesh to achieve a resurrection for man's sake with the promised hope of a new life arising transcending death. Thus the *Book of the Dead*, though treating death with all the awe attendant on it, yet presented death as a passage to new life. People, as the custom was, had their tear bottles and wept genuine tears for the dead, yet not with the depth of tragedy of later times.

The impression is that the Egyptians were in the main a happy, even a gay people. They had 'their solemn ceremonial occasions but also their festive times with pipe and tabor, dance and song, for both occasions as appropriate. Egypt was a land of art and also of crafts for the further embellishment of life. It had its science too, after its kind, a knowledge of the stars, of medicine and healing, of the earth and nature in her circling seasons, through which they read the language of the gods. Religion, art and science, for what they were, had not yet separated and were in happy communion with one another.

But then there was always the great Mother Nile also, descending from a divine source and providing all the resources for a thriving agriculture, in which men and women alongside one another could by their joint labours provide for the daily bread. Thus, at its best, it was a well-rounded life.

It is remarkable to think that the birth of Egyptian culture five thousand years ago and all the grandeur it achieved coincided with humanity's entry into Kali Juga, the age of greatest spiritual darkness. Yet, seen from today, Egypt was steeped through and through with spirituality. Its temples were mystery centres and schools of initiation in which the Pharaoh-to-be took at least some part in preparation for his high office. With priest-initiates as his counsellors, he was elevated to be the supreme ego for the whole people. His word was unquestionable law. We see him, as in the sculptured forms that have come down to us, sitting straight-backed, his legs somewhat parted as though ready to spring to the upright, his feet firmly planted on the ground, his eyes gazing into distances beyond the visible, doves at his ears, as divine messengers, whispering secrets to him intended for him alone. It was thus he ruled. It was thus the great pyramids were built by the massed labourers file on file. This is the image at its highest. Later came times of confusion and decline, but also voices foretelling a time to come when the great Sun-Spirit would have other words to speak to men.

The pyramids were tombs envisaging how the discarnate soul of the deceased ruler, in mounting it, left the weight of earth and the earthly behind him. At the peak of the pyramid, substance vanished and the soul, as though in an inverted pyramid of light, continued its ascent into the widening heavens, even to the stars which carried the secrets of all and everything.

In contrast to this was the strange practice of the embalming of the dead. This, Rudolf Steiner tells us, had the effect of keeping the soul more closely inclined towards the earth. Then, in the subsequent incarnation, it would be all the more ready to descend more deeply into matter leading to the materialistic outlook with its mastery of the physical.

We have yet to consider the great enigmatic figure of the Sphinx, raised above the sands, calling on man even now as it did then, to solve the riddle of his own existence. There it stands, silent now, though legend tells there were times when it emitted sounds. What power of imagination built it out of the four apocalyptic beasts so vividly described three thousand years later in the Book of Revelation, yet already forevisioned by Zarathustra and here united into one mighty form: the great wings of the eagle, the powerful chest of the lion, the fiery force of the bull, and then the human countenance, presaging the threefold man not yet descended. The Sphinx of Egypt gazes into a future when the archetypal being of man will stand openly revealed – *Ecce Homo*!

Ancient Greece

And now, still moving forward in time, we come to the Graeco-Roman, the fourth cultural epoch. This epoch extended to the end of the Middle Ages, but it is Greece we need particularly to consider in terms of advancing human consciousness. We can only select a few significant features from the epics, the dramas, and the philosophy. Greece opens up a totally new chapter in man's experience of himself and the world.

First, then, in regard to the *Iliad*; the two outstanding figures are Hector and Achilles. They epitomize, by their different natures, the characters of the opposing armies. Achilles is of the younger race, the Greek, violent in his love and hate, able to sulk when offended, but in action moving with a proud impetuosity that nothing can restrain. Because he felt wronged by Agamemnon he refused to accompany his beloved friend Patroclus into battle, but then when he heard that Patroclus had been killed by a death blow from Hector, his rage against Hector knew no bounds. Hector belonged to an old race, depicted in the figure of aged Priam, his father. Hector is as valiant as Achilles, but wise and forbearing. He moves forward with quiet resolve, prepared to look destiny in the face despite forebodings of death. He is killed by Achilles whom nothing else would satisfy but that his body should be thrown to the dogs to be mutilated by them and torn apart. Only the kneeling figure of Priam is able to dissuade him.

But now, there is a background to this battle of the two heroes. The gods are active in it, Apollo on behalf of Hector, and Pallas Athene, determined that Achilles must win. Their fate has been decided already by decree of Jove. In the narrative Pallas Athene actually befools Hector so that he loses his guard. In the end then it is a duel between Apollo, a sun being, and Pallas Athene sprung from the brow of Jove. It is her mission to foster a new force of intelligence. She is the inspirer of the Greek art of philosophy. The warm heart of Apollo pleading for Hector has to give way. The old must die that the new may be born. The Greeks, impetuous, virile, young, by confronting a dying culture come to a new stage of consciousness out of which to mould their future. Helen for whom they fought is the embodiment of the beauty that will shape their art. The

Trojans, in encountering the youthfulness of the Greeks, though defeated in battle, receive an impulse of renewed life which, through Aeneas, will flow into shaping the future of Rome. Men are still the fulfillers of the will of Gods and not yet fully themselves.

The whole of the Graeco-Trojan war which is part mythical, part historical, rages around the figure of Helen of Troy. According to the legend, Paris, a son of old Priam and brother of Hector, had actually abducted her from Greece where she belonged. Her beauty, renowned through all time since, is of a divine-human character expressed in all that is beauty in nature and in human creativity. It is for this that the Greeks fought. Paris hoped she would be the means of renewing the life and culture of dying Troy. For the Greeks she was to be the embodiment of all that was to flower as beauty in Greek art and culture. Hence they were to be called Hellenes, and Greek art, Hellenic Art.

Here is an example of how the tales of antiquity carry within them a depth of meaning far beyond the external rational. So, too, Pallas Athene who sprang into being from the forehead of Jove, was the embodiment of the new faculty of thought as Greek philosophy, hence the city of Athens is named after her, and to be an Athenian meant to be specially endowed with the gift of her being. All the Greek heroes and heroines, including the divine Apollo bore something of this divine or semi-divine character.

The nearest term we have in modern usage may be in the word genius. Amongst its several meanings, the Oxford dictionary includes, supernatural being, exalted intellectual power, instinctive and extraordinary, creative and inventive capacity.

What we are attempting in this brief survey of the culture epochs is to try and capture a sense of how the faculty of imagination or spiritual vision changed from epoch to epoch; or we could also say, how truth spoke to the heart of man.

Ulysses is the third main figure in the Iliad. He is described as *cunning*. By the subterfuge of the wooden horse, the Trojans are lured out of the fastness of their city walls to their downfall. This same Ulysses is the hero of the Odyssey. There we see his intelligence take other forms. We see him embarking on a voyage of perilous adventures; he passes through the dangers of Scylla and Charybdis; by a cunning ruse he defeats the one-eyed Cyclops that would devour him; he escapes the beguiling singing of the Sirens, and overcomes the witchery of Circe. He crosses the dread river Styx to reach at last the bournes of Hades and have communion with the dead bringing back from there new guiding forces for the living. He returns a wanderer in disguise to his home, in fact a new man, to disperse the crowd of lying aspirants, the hungry lusts and passions that assail his consort Penelope who, by her courage, faith and constancy, no lesser trials than his, had held the way open for his return as initiate guide to his people. In this wondrous tale of initiation we recognize the far-seeing vision of 'blind Homer'.

In connection with Greek drama we will confine ourselves to the theme of Orestes. The following are the circumstances. Agamemnon, to appease the angry waves which threatened his ships on the way to Troy, sacrificed his daughter Iphigenia. After ten years he returns home a victor, but Clytemnestra, his wife, in revenge for the death of their daughter, has him murdered. Orestes, their son, is on a journey. Suddenly he is confronted by the furious Erinnyes, the shades of his dead father, demanding revenge on their part. Bound by the old law, he has no other recourse. He returns home and brings about the death of his mother. But now it is her shades that pursue him, giving him no peace. Where is he to go? He flees to the temple of Pallas Athene, pleading for her intervention on his behalf. Whose is the guilt? That is the question to be resolved. The shades of Clytemnestra will not be appeased and demand vengeance. Apollo appears and a dialogue ensues between him and Pallas Athene. Again these two gods confront each other as opposites, the former defending the old law of retribution, of pity for the victim, the latter with her philosophic vision, intent on finding a new solution. In the end she invites twelve citizens of Athens to form a court of justice. Apollo and Pallas Athene plead their causes. The citizens' votes divide equally. Then Pallas Athene, since Orestes had sought help in her temple, gives the casting vote in his favour. The unending era of tragedy following tragedy is broken. Orestes is set free. A new day has dawned. The fearful aged Erinnyes are transformed into beautiful temple maidens singing a new found song of hope and harmony for the future.

The author, many years ago, produced a version of this play with the older scholars of the Rudolf Steiner School, New York. The effect of the end scene was deeply moving. It was like a premonition of the resurrection scene at Easter, ·the weight of death overcome and a new life begun. This was the work of Aeschylus.

Euripides, his younger contemporary, wrote a drama on the same theme. Already the supersensible element is more veiled. In Euripides, Orestes is no longer pursued by spectres. Instead, he is lying on a couch in torment, attacked from within. Rudolf Steiner draws attention to the fact that here we have the actual moment of the birth of conscience. What had been experienced clairvoyantly from outside has vanished to become interiorized as conscience, and this profound change takes place within the lifetime of an older and a younger contemporary.

Perhaps the greatest innovation in Greek culture is the birth of philosophy, a word combining love and wisdom. With the entry of philosophy we have reached a stage in human progress when the older pictorial consciousness withdraws and instead it is thoughts to which we are accustomed, but thoughts endowed with life, so that the idea world is a real world in which we are at home. We may recall the death scene of Socrates. Some of his closest disciples were with him when the attendant entered with the poison he was to take. He had been condemned, accused of misleading the young and drawing them away from the old gods. Actually he was trying to wean them from relying in their judgements on mere instinct and inborn habits. Having taken the poison, he continued with his calm discourse, remarking at one point that the cold was creeping up his limbs and would presently reach the heart. Some who were present wept. Socrates reproved them gently. Did they not yet realize that the philosopher all through life is striving to die to the allurements of the world of the senses in order to reach the realm of immortal values, the realm of ideas? Why then weep because he is leaving for the home he has sought for all through life.

For Plato, for Socrates, the world of ideas is also the world of ideals. Thus Socrates taught of the four great ideals or virtues, Wisdom, Justice, Courage, Temperance, most remarkably the same ideals that had taken outer form in the caste system of India thousands of years before. What had once given rise outwardly to a great social structure was now reborn ideally from within. In such a transition from outer to inner guidance we begin to sense the true meaning of human history.

Aristotle carried experience a stage further. He sought for the idea in its outer manifestation in nature. This established him as the guiding spirit in science for two thousand years. He still was able to see the outer world with inner perception. For those who lack that inner eye, Aristotle, as scientist, is wholly discredited. Galileo rejected him utterly.

Aristotle was the teacher of Alexander the Great, born the night that the mystery centre at Ephesus was destroyed by an act of arson. Rudolf Steiner describes it as a wonderful esoteric school for men and women alike. The teachings given there related much to the mystery of the word as though in preparation for the greatest mystery to come – "and the word was made flesh and dwelt among us". By the time of Alexander, spiritual knowledge was already much on the wane. His mission was not, as is often supposed, for outer conquests, but to establish centres where knowledge of the divine could be resuscitated. There was great emptiness of soul everywhere. There is a legend about Caesar Augustus, the greatest of the Caesars. He was about to be deified by his people when he saw a vision of a child born in Bethlehem, the King of Kings. Paul in the Acts describes how he and Barnabas were hailed as the returned Mercury and Jupiter. On Paul denying this, the people there were so enraged that they had much ado to escape from being stoned to death. To such a low ebb had life in the spirit sunk.

The fourth post-Atlantean culture epoch covers an immense range of events: the rise of Christianity; the decline of Rome; the rise of Islam; the Crusades; the great monastic schools; the great cathedrals; the mediaeval walled cities; Church supremacy, the feudal system, and the ensuing struggle between Church and State; the Troubadours, the mediaeval guilds, the miracle and mystery plays at the Christian festivals, folk-lore and song and dance – and so much else. Yet with all the changes, man looked to the stars as to the homes of heavenly intelligences, and felt the earth to be the centre of it all. The Ptolemaic view of the world ruled everywhere. Thus there was a common ground of outlook from Homer to Dante – they stood at opposite ends of a single epoch. By contrast, from Dante to Copernicus, with little more than a century between, the change of outlook was startlingly great. The world was stood on its head. It is that change that brings us into the fifth post-Atlantean epoch in which we now are.

The Fifth Epoch

Beginning from 1413, when the sun first entered the constellation of the fishes, we are still, as an epoch, very young with fifteen hundred years more to go. Obedience, whether to Church or State, had been the prevailing rule. To question the powers divine was sacrilege, to question government, a form of treason. The age we are in is one where everything is questioned. It is a questioning age, and everything is undergoing such rapid change that it is well-nigh impossible to prognosticate what life on earth will be like a hundred years from now, let alone fifteen hundred years still to come. Life swung into the fifth epoch with great impetus. There was the burst into Renaissance Christian art; the birth of a new age of poetry and drama; the exploration of the seas and the discovery of a new world, not only North and South America, but South Africa, and later Australia and New Zealand – life on earth had suddenly expanded. Then there was also the Reformation, not in one but in many places, and the new art of printing which made the Bible available in the vernacular – that, too, was a great expansion of its own kind. But if we are to characterize the age quite particularly, the mind goes back to Galileo, the founder of the age of science. He stood much alone in his life time and ended his days in strict confinement under the orders of the Church. To him we ascribe three main innovations. We can do little more than name them. First, he established the law of gravitation from his study of falling bodies, later developed further by Newton. As a consequence, the laws of inertia, of the motion of lifeless objects, took possession of the human mind also in regard to the heavens, driving all spiritual considerations into the background. The stars and the planets and the earth itself went dead.

Secondly, with the telescope he himself had made, he confirmed, what even to Copernicus was still only a surmise, that the earth was a spinning top going round the sun, and that the sun itself rotated round an axis – everything conceived mechanically.

The third and most subtle influence to be ascribed to

Galileo, and the one that has affected most deeply man's view of himself and the world, lies in his division of human experience into two distinct categories, the quantitative and the qualitative. He was the first to formulate this, though it was adopted by Newton (who was born the day Galileo died), and by the world of science generally, down to today. Expressed in his own terms, in regard to "a piece of matter or corporeal substance" he felt as *real* the fact that, "in its own nature it is bounded and figured in such and such a figure, that in relation to others it is large or small, that it is in this or that place, in this or that time, that it is in motion or remains at rest, that it touches or does not touch another body, that it is single, few or many." These are the qualities he sees as real and pertaining to the object in question. On the other hand, whether the same "piece of matter or corporeal substance" is deemed "white or red, bitter or sweet, sounding or mute, of a pleasant or unpleasant odour," – such qualities for Galileo only "seem to exist". They do not actually pertain to the object "but hold their residence solely in the sensible body; so that if the animal were removed, every such quality would be abolished and annihilated." This is an astonishing phenomenon, the more so for its having captured the mind and captivated man in himself. Henceforth only phenomena that submit to numerical treatment, such as weight, measure, number, motion, in other words only quantitative values are to be regarded as objectively valid for scientific investigation. All other values that engage the sensations, feelings, or any other response of an inward character, the qualitative aspect of experience, is declared subjective and of no validity in determining the nature of the world. In this way the whole life of inner experience touching art, religion, moral idealism, indeed, man himself as regards his humanity is set to one side. The soul of man is split in two. As one twentieth century thinker, Alexis Carrell expressed it half a century ago, it is this view that had led to the triumph of technology and the degradation of man.

It is not that Galileo in his own life adhered only to his view of the physical world. All the evidence shows him to have remained at all times a devotee of the Catholic Church despite the way it treated him, for it condemned his work and held him under conditions of solitary confinement, admitting visitors only under sanction. Such a visitor, when Galileo was already old and blind and working on his magnum opus in physics, was the as yet young poet Milton. Galileo could still live naively and contentedly in two worlds, the physical world of the senses as he saw it, and the religious world of faith. He could not have foreseen that he had set in train something that was to lead to scepticism, agnosticism, atheism and eventually to scientific material-ism and that the prelates who opposed him had an uneasy premonition of where his science was to lead.

We have enlarged on this third innovation of Galileo because it so plainly concerns the present day.

The physics which the genius of Galileo released has led to all reliance being placed on the quantitative making the qualitative secondary and ephemeral. Physics has affected biology, and that again psychology, reducing man to becoming a phantom of himself.

In this way there came the split between the humanities and the sciences. After all, Shakespeare was born in the same year as Galileo, in 1564. He took as his dominion just the one that science left out of account, the dominion of the intrinsically human. There has been a great company of poets, artists, thinkers, who have sought to construct their own world where measurement cannot apply, – a world which is very real in terms of experience. Even Galileo, himself, was a good musician as well as a scientist, showing that men remain human, whatever their theories. But that which was the morality and the faith of the past no longer had any ground under it.

The other outstanding feature of the past five centuries is

that of emancipation from authority of any kind in a search
for personal freedom. First, with the Reformation, came
the demand for freedom of belief. Then came the revolt
against monarchical rule, in France the great Revolution, in
England the civil war between the Royalists and the Roundheads ending with the beheading of Charles I, regarded
still by many as a martyr. The idea of democracy was born.
Kingship, as constitutional monarchy, where it lingers on,
has the virtue of standing beyond political parties.

And now, in this century particularly, the struggle has
been and still is to find a new basis for economic life.

With priest, ruler, and merchant in the earlier form laid
aside, what is left of the ancient castes but the Sudra, the
fourth and humblest. We are in a real sense all Sudras seen in
the light of the threefold commonwealth: each has to be
priest to himself or choose his own priest in freedom; each
ideally has his part as ruler in the democratic life of rights;
each has his responsibility, according to his endowments, to
the economic life. What then is the task of the Sudra? Who is
the Sudra but the individual ego? Seen this way, the whole
trend is towards a threefold commonwealth.

A parapsychologist once asked the author: what evidence
is there of real human progress? The only answer he could
give was that in the past responsibility rested on the few
whereas today it rests on each and all.

To ignore this results inevitably in states of unfreedom.
This brings us back to the question, what it is that constitutes freedom, and to the further question, by what do
human beings really live? It is clear that the crises which
meet us are reflections of the crisis in ourselves. There never
can be or will be outer freedom until men have found the
ground of inner freedom. Sometimes the truth of this
comes in very unexpected ways.

A writer, describing the experiences of some of the
Russian dissidents, gave instances of how, under conditions
of extreme physical and mental torture, if only they could

find the inner resistance to hold on, determined by an indefinable faith not to give way, a miracle could occur. A point could be reached where one was filled with an unassailable peace, with compassion even for the persecutors as being the weaker, with forgiveness and the absolute certainty that in the end the world was ruled and life determined, whatever the outer pressures, by mysterious powers from within. There was a source within which remained unassailable.

Extending this more widely to the world of today, one might say: never has humanity been so wildly distracted, never so beset with mental, moral, physical threats and dangers, nor exposed to such widespread division and distrust. Never has the individual felt so abandoned in his loneliness, never so tempted to see himself as a nonentity, yet never has he been brought more fully to realize that he is indeed a *self* and that it is on this discovery that the future of the world depends. Never has he heard so clearly the call from within: "Man know thyself". It is this awakening call that, despite all the negatives, is spreading through the world to declare in this age of contradictions what man truly is. It is the character of the age that has brought anthroposophy into our time, not to revive old faiths, but to bring a new knowledge of man to inspire new faith.

Man has lost the world of the spirit in order that he may in all freedom find the spirit in himself and, finding the spirit in himself, discover the spirit in the world anew but now as a fully conscious member of the whole.

Thus far has our search for the meaning of history brought us. We still have to find the underlying force that carries us forward.

A Time of Testing

The Child as Guide

WE FIND OURSELVES endowed with a certain type of consciousness. This is not what we are born with. Our children tell us that. They make us aware how hard it is to enter the mind of childhood. The younger the child the more difficult it is. We can still hold reasonable converse with our adolescents, partly because we still recollect something of our own youth and how differently we then reacted to life. In the eyes of youth we often appear as failures. They see all too clearly how little we are able to cope with life. Deep in their feelings there still lives a faith that can move mountains – not as they see us move them with dynamite or other explosives. That leaves them impressed in a way but unmoved. They carry an inner knowledge that the world should be better than it is. In the depths of their being, they are seekers for truth. They want to discover and are glad to be helped to discover that there are real goals in life and that the world is built on truth. Yet where is this truth to be found? How are they to recognize it? Truth must be truth. They are not fond of compromise. The feeling for what lives beyond the rational is what they really live by, and without this there can be no art and no religion and in the end nothing to live for. There are truths in life, those that touch us most deeply, that can be grasped only by an act of imagination, – what might be described as a dreaming coming from a higher source. That is what people still possessed naturally in the fourth post-Atlantean epoch. And that is what we adults as a rule no longer possess. When the man of today says 'I' to himself, he feels secure in his physical body – the brain is also body. That was not so for the Greek. He still felt himself one with the life of nature, one with nature. Rudolf Steiner tells us, for example, that the Greek sculptor had no need of a model. He still sensed the plastic formative or etheric forces that had shaped his own body and he could work out of these. He felt them objectively, therefore in early Greece art was not yet personalized. Jove, Apollo, Homer, Socrates, they bore the same likenesses no matter who the sculptors were. This is quite different in Christian art where each artist offers his own interpretation. The Greek, for example, could still experience the essential nature of the four elements: fire was hot and dry, air was warm and wet, water was cold and wet, earth was cold and dry. By these qualities he could judge the regions of the earth; he could also judge people in their dispositions and temperaments. The elemental nature spirits still were live and vivid in the folk imagination. They had their allotted places and their tasks. They lived not only in Greece but in that epoch of time in many places. The gnomes could hammer sunlight into gold, (the dwarf Regan in the Norse myth for example), moonlight into silver, they invisibly cut the crystal forms, but they were also busy where the plant was rooted in the earth. The undines of the watery element were to be met in the sparkling streams and brooks and mountain waterways but also in the sap of stem and leaf at the unfolding of the plant. The airy sylphs, said Rudolf Steiner, taught the birds their songs, but they also brought colour into the world in the opening bud and the crowning flower. And the flashing sparkling salamanders rejoiced in the mounting flames but also shot their secret fire into the forming seeds to give them power of expansion when the next sun season came. The great Italian sculptor Benvenuto Cellini tells in his autobiography how as a child he saw a salamander and how he ran to tell his father and how his father gave him a sound thrashing to knock such nonsense out of his head. No wonder that children have got so shy of telling things. How cold our nature would have been to those ancients.

To the Greeks, to see Pallas Athene or Apollo or some other god appear upon the stage was natural, but the human actors were disguised behind masks and wore high-heeled shoes to give them added stature – as humans they were not yet fully descended to the earth, not yet personalities born. The heroes stood midway between gods and humans, they were offspring of a divine being and a mortal.

How then, at that time, did they experience the 'I'? When Socrates needed to solve a problem he retired to a lonely spot – he could stand for hours in deepest contemplation, communing with his *daemon*, with his higher self. What was this higher self other than his immortal nature, his ego, not yet fully incarnated. If this were understood, we would know better how to listen to our present-day adolescents, for though present conditions of incarnation are different and the environment too is different, yet at their stage they are till Greek in soul – they are not yet fully earth-born for the dream force from pre-birth is still active within them. Whether they act for good or ill largely depends on what meets them in the adult world; they still are living as in dream, therefore not yet wholly responsible. They teach us that without the faculty of imagination life is barren. If we wish to enter truly into the Greek world, the adolescent tells us we must develop imagination, not fancifulness but what we might call a perceptive faculty that carries further than the obvious.

And now, if we are to go back to pre-adolescence, to childhood proper, how are we to convey our meaning to a twelve-year-old, a nine-year-old, a six-year-old? There is only one way; we have to become poets like the bards of old to sing heroic tales to their listening ears, for then they *will* listen. This is no exaggeration. They want to listen to us from inside, to hear the word within the word, the True Word as it echoes back from within themselves from their life before birth. Out of where is our speaking born? What is it wanting to come to utterance through us? Nothing for the young child has yet become commonplace and ordinary; if it has, then as children they are displaced to become premature adults. We need to have resort to the magic of the legend, the fable, the story, the more than real. At their stage all life is a parable – we offer the picture and the meaning will dawn for them in time. Truth for them is not yet in the idea but in the language of the picture. We need to know that children in these years live by the force of inspiration. That is their mode of experiencing, though they themselves could never say it. Inspiration is related to the ear as imagination is to the eye. Happy is the teacher who can really reach the child through the power of the word. From this love springs naturally. The Magi *saw* the star, and that is how our adolescents need to see. The shepherds *heard* the words and that is how our children need to *hear* – the word which gives assurance 'to men of goodwill' of a world built on peace and harmony, and the beauty this gives rise to.

And now, looking back in history, how did the people of the third epoch, the Egyptian people of that time live? By seeing, yes, but essentially by hearing, by listening to the word of authority which guided them in shaping their lives: they heard the word of Pharaoh, and he heard the word of his counsellors, the initiate priests, and they heard what the gods had to tell. After death they listened to the words of Osiris as he summed up their previous lives and revealed the future. The ear is a more ancient and intimate organ than the eye.

Going back to the second post-Atlantean culture epoch and to Zarathustra, all is dialogue, is direct utterance of the Sun-God Ahura Mazdao in answer to the questioning voice of Zarathustra; and what he heard he conveyed as instruction to his listening people, to shape their lives accordingly. He was the one great mediator between the folk and their God and the power of the word was even more immediate. It is through the word that we can cultivate the faculty of inspiration which has its source in a life of dialogue before birth.

How can we hope to understand the Middle Ages, then going back to Greece, to Egypt and to Persia, with our intellectualized analytical minds of today. It is the child in these middle years and earlier that, by his response or unresponsiveness can guide us. One can hear without listening but one cannot listen without hearing.

And now going back still further to the first post-Atlantean culture epoch, to Ancient India, the priests conveyed their teachings out of higher realms to which they had access. The Seven Holy Rishis reached heights from which the words they brought worked as magical powers, as the will of God. This they conveyed to the people. "Thy will be done." So it is with children in their infant years – it is not the words as words that reach them but what lives as disposition of heart and will in our words – it is this that teaches them, and what lives as moral force in our actions. It is this, not the mere outer gesture, that they imitate and by doing so become one with us. Imitation for the little child is not just copying. They live by the force of intuition which is beyond the picture and the word, beyond imagination and inspiration. It is here that we reach the meaning of, "except ye become as little children, ye cannot enter the kingdom of heaven." There is utmost tenderness but also profoundest depth in such a saying.

Further back in time, the child is still in heaven, preparing to descend to earth. It is thus the understanding of the child can guide us – the younger the child, the higher must we mount in spirit to reach him. And the further we go back in the history and prehistory of mankind, there too, the earlier the stage the higher must we ascend in consciousness to meet the need of the people of that time. We should not speak of primitive peoples but of *earlier* peoples. And when

we go back into early Lemurian times, it is as with the child
before birth, humanity has not yet descended to earth but is
biding the time allotted to it. It is crass foolishness to think
that modern man has arisen out of previous states of barbar-
ism and savagery. If such have been found they are merely
evidence of degeneracy from conditions where law and
custom under divine and human guidance once prevailed.

Christ and the Human Ego

Biologically, despite all the differences that exist and have
existed between the peoples of the earth, humanity is one.
Whereas all the animal types divide into species, the mam-
mal into eighty thousand, the insects into over a million,
even the primates divide, humanity remains one species. It
follows then that all the changes of consciousness we have
been describing are progressive changes in the one being,
Man. Though in each epoch there has been a dominant
people, yet, despite variation in degree of participation, in
the overall development humanity continues to remain
single. On what, then, is this oneness grounded? Even as
the human ego penetrates all parts of the human organism
and makes of all that diversity of members, organs, tissues,
functions an all containing unity, where shall we look for
the corresponding unifying source in regard to all the separate peoples?

We recall the words of Saint Paul. His contention was that
Christ had come for all men, not for one particular people,
as some supposed.

Now there are diversities of gifts, but the same Spirit.
And there are differences of administration, but the
same Lord.
And there are diversities of operations, but it is the
same God which worketh all in all.
But the manifestation of the Spirit is given to every
man to profit withal.

For as the body is one, and hath many members and all the members of that one body, being many, are one body: so also is Christ.

For by one Spirit are we all baptized into one body, whether we be Jews or Gentiles, whether we be bond or free; and have been all made to drink into one Spirit.

I CORINTHIANS 12:4

What Paul is saying is that all the different peoples with their different gifts and capacities are individual members of the one humanity imbued with one Spirit, with one uniting Ego. Out of his experience at Damascus he proclaims that that one Spirit belonging to all is Christ, the Messiah for all mankind.

The Christ Paul speaks of is beyond all separate religions and churches, (by whatever name they may be called), and beyond all division into sects and sections. The One includes the All whilst denying nothing to each particular. And so it is also with anthroposophy for its teaching is directed to each and all without distinction.

When the author first came to anthroposophy and began to read the basic books, *Knowledge of Higher Worlds*, *Theosophy*, and others, he wondered why there was no mention of Christ. Even in *Occult Science* we meet the name first in connection with the Atlantean mysteries. Later he came to see that just as Rudolf Steiner's many lectures on the Gospels were given out of the experiences he had had before ever he had read them, so he offered a wide range of spiritual studies and, indeed, a whole new cosmology in order to help us approach newly what is the very heart centre of anthroposophy as Christianity, freed from traditions and any form of partisanship.

Then history, too, acquires its real meaning. By degrees we learn to understand that the Word, the Logos, the Being who came to be known as Christ, has been the guiding spirit of human evolution from all times, and that Christianity, therefore, has room in it for all religions.

From spiritual heights, He has accompanied man in his descent into matter, reaching him and upholding him through the mystery schools of all the ages where He is known as the ruling Spirit of the Sun. He is the Light, the Life, the Spirit of Love as these stream through all existences. We recall that it was the great initiate of the Sun Oracle in Atlantis who led his disciples eastward and there, in western Asia, created a spiritual centre from which the guidance was given for all the successive cultural epochs we have described. The Christ was united with all of them. In Ancient India He manifested as Vishnu who ever and again sent Krishna down to intervene in times of crisis. Krishna in his teachings calls on man to grow more conscious as a Self. He thus prepares the way for the one who will be the bringer of the I AM. In Ancient Persia He manifests as Ahura Mazdao, directing man through Zarathustra to take stronger hold of earth existence and himself. In Egypt, Osiris the Sun-God, through his death and his restoration to the spiritual worlds prepares the souls of men for the greatest of all events to come, the descent of Christ Himself. To Moses He appears as the burning bush. In answer to the question, "Who shall I say sent me," came the words, "Say the I AM sent you." In Greece Apollo reflects the inner nature of the Sun even as Helios reflects its outer nature so that the inner spiritual and the outer physical, like everything else typifying Greek culture, are held in balance. In this whole history Buddha, in his last incarnation as a Bodhisattva, living about five hundred years before Christ had a great world mission to fulfil. He was the teacher of compassion not only for all men but for all life on this earth. By 'eliminating' the caste system from his teaching he places the onus simply on each individual and this, in itself, prepares for the free and independent position of the individual based on the experience of the I AM. Alexander in his journeys and the founding of centres for the renewing of spiritual culture prepares the way for the all-world impulse of Christ. And then comes the announcement of John the Baptist, "The kingdom of Heaven is at hand." Christ repeats this. Later Christ says, "My kingdom is not of this world." Rudolf Steiner interprets the kingdom as the I AM which Christ brings to mankind, whereby from children of God they may become brothers in Christ. It was at the time when the mysteries were most shrouded that Christ incarnated, bringing the revelation of himself into outer perceptible form.

> He was in the world, and the world was made by him, and the world knew him not.
> He came unto his own, and his own received him not.

And then the words:

> But as many as received him, to them gave he power to become Sons of God, even to them that believe in his name;
> Which were born, not of blood, nor of the will of the flesh, nor of the will of man, but of God.

Who then are to be the sons of God? They who are able to receive into themselves the new-born power of the I AM, and who thus, henceforth, can grow to the godhead now within them – they who in future, through the deed of the Christ become man, will, through the endowment of the I AM, draw the creative powers of renewing light and life and love for the world from within themselves. It is thus we can interpret the words of Paul, "Not I but Christ in me", not what the world has made of me, but what I, having received the I AM, must now make of myself and the world. Whereas, before the coming of Christ, one sought for the self in higher worlds, since the coming of Christ, each one, looking into himself, can truly say with Him, the I AM that I find in myself is not of this world but my task is here. Through Christ becoming man, every human being today should be able to incarnate more completely, should be more truly man on earth than ever he was before. How is it that the understanding of the mystery of Golgotha, the death and the resurrection, has, as we have seen, grown dimmer, and that man, instead of finding himself an immortal nature fulfilling a high destiny on his planet earth, has lost the meaning of destiny, and indeed of his own existence? It is this we have to explore more fully. The broad history was given in the section on Kali-yuga but now we must turn to the actual influences at work. On the other hand, it is in surmounting the trials and obstacles which man is obliged to meet that man can hope to grow to his full estate.

The Adversaries

One cannot go far into Spiritual Science without coming to realize that adverse spiritual powers, powers of hindrance and opposition, do actually exist and are active. It is their will to deflect humanity from its rightful course of development and thus to defeat the mission of Christ.

Christopher Marlowe, born in 1564, the same year as Shakespeare and Galileo, wrote a play, *Doctor Faustus*, on this very theme. Goethe knew the play and admired it. His *Faust* has a very similar opening.

Faustus is an accomplished scholar in several fields, Aristotelian logic, philosophy, medicine, and even theology. He is a frustrated figure, for with all his accomplishments he is no more than an ordinary man. Learning can take him no further and so he turns to necromancy, and ignoring all warnings begins to practise magic.

Mephistopheles appears, the father of lies, and inveigles Faustus into signing a contract with his own blood for a period of twenty-four years. During this time Mephistopheles will hold himself at the bidding of Faustus in all things. His blood congeals. But Mephistopheles fetches 'a chafer of coles' to dissolve it back. The blood rises against

the deed, forms the words *Homo fuge* – his own blood bids
him flee but he ignores it.

Faustus becomes a court magician, he can perform amazing engineering feats, can invent a flying ship to India to
fetch grapes for the Duchess in the midst of winter. He
brings about a wonder. With Mephistopheles at his side he
calls up the shape of Helen –

> Was this the face that launcht a thousand shippes
> And burnt the toplesse Towres of Ilium?

All this he can do, but he wants more. He wants to
penetrate to the mysteries, to know what rules in the stars,
what is heaven, what hell, but finds that Mephistopheles
can only mouth the barren nothings he is all too familiar
with already. He sees now he has been deceived. Curses will
not help. He falls into a state of deepest gloom. Mephistopheles, alarmed lest he break his contract, fetches Lucifer,
who comes leading in his trail all the seven vices to drown
the soul of Faust and glut his appetites. This fails, too, for it
offers him no answers.

The play proceeds. The final hour has come. The clock
has struck eleven. Time moves on.

> The devil will come, and Faustus must be damnd.
> O Ile leap up to my Gods: who pulles me down?
> See see where Christ's blood streams in the firmament
> One drop would save my soule, halfe a drop, ah my
> > Christ!

It does not take much to see that Marlowe was a modern
spirit, ultra-modern in his time. The sheriffs were on their
way to arrest him as an atheist! He was killed in a tavern
brawl.

What astonishes is that Marlowe sees Christ's deed as not
for the earth only but that it reaches to the far universe.

Marlowe was modern in another sense too. He broke the fetters of the old rhymed couplet and bequeathed on the English language his 'mighty line' of blank verse which Shakespeare carried to such magnificent bounds – the line on which the greatest in English poetry was to be built.

We have in him one who stood at the threshold of this modern age and saw with amazing fore-vision the dangers that lay ahead – and at the same time still had knowledge of the two great adversaries, Mephistopheles and Lucifer.

Lucifer and Mephistopheles-Ahriman have been known through the ages in their different guises: Lucifer as a red-headed, dancing mischievous devil; Ahriman, dark, sinister, threatening, Satanic; Lucifer as tempter of the soul; Ahriman as the deceiver, the falsifier of the spirit; Lucifer as pride, Ahriman as greed. Both appear in a host of folk-legends. But both are also known in the mystery schools, now one taking prominence, now the other. In Ancient India it was Lucifer taking the lead, in Ancient Persia, Ahriman; Lucifer in his mystical trends away from the Earth veers more towards the East; Ahriman spelling out earthly Utopias, leans more to the West. Lucifer and Ahriman, once we know them, are found active everywhere. It is wholly understandable, therefore, that the first experience of Christ after his descent into the sheaths of Jesus at the baptism was his encounter with them in the scene of the 'wilderness' which Rudolf Steiner translates as 'loneliness'. This scene is described almost identically in Matthew and Luke, is only hinted at in Mark with mention of 'wild beasts', and does not appear in John.

In Matthew 4:1-11 it reads as follows:

Then was Jesus led up of the Spirit into the wilderness to be tempted of the devil.

And when he had fasted forty days and forty nights, he was afterward an hungred

And when the tempter came to him, he said, If thou be

the Son of God, command that these stones be made bread.

But he answered and said, It is written, Man shall not live by bread alone, but by every word that proceedeth out of the mouth of God.

Then the devil taketh him up into the holy city, and setteth him on a pinnacle of the temple,

And saith unto him, If thou be the Son of God, cast thyself down: for it is written, He shall give his angels charge concerning thee: and in their hands they shall bear thee up, lest at any time thou dash thy foot against a stone.

Jesus said unto him, It is written again, Thou shalt not tempt the Lord thy God.

Again, the devil taketh him up into an exceeding high mountain, and sheweth him all the kingdoms of the world, and the glory of them;

And saith unto him, All these things will I give thee, if thou wilt fall down and worship me.

Then said Jesus unto him, Get thee hence Satan, for it is written, Thou shalt worship the Lord thy God, and him only shalt thou serve.

Then the devil leaveth him, and behold angels came and ministered unto him.

In both Gospels the temptation of the turning of the stones into bread comes first. In Luke the order of the other two is reversed.

Rudolf Steiner sees working in this scene both Lucifer and Ahriman.

He places first the scene of the 'exceeding high mountain' and ascribes this to Lucifer "who draws near to men when they prize the self too highly and are lacking in humility and self-knowledge." His aim is to play on self-pride and self-glorification.

The second temptation, that of the high pinnacle he

ascribes jointly to Lucifer and Ahriman. "Lucifer sought to goad His pride; Ahriman, to play upon His fear." Since their ambitions are opposite they annulled each other.

In regard to the third test, that of turning stones into bread, there Ahriman acts alone. Christ, never having lived on earth, could not have known how men change stones, mineral substance, that is, money into bread. Ahriman uses this to his advantage. Christ who could say, "I am the bread of life", is later betrayed for thirty pieces of silver.

Christ overcame Lucifer by entering into the blood of man and purging it of every taint of egotism. Hence, in the legend of the Holy Grail, this blood, gathered by Joseph of Arimathea as it flowed from the side of Christ into the cup of the Last Supper, becomes the chalice bringing healing and the power of transubstantiation to the soul. Ahriman he defeats by overcoming death through the resurrection. It is left to man in his freedom to unite himself with the deeds of Christ. Until his descent to the earth Christ guided humanity from outside as a God. Now by receiving through Christ the Kingdom of Heaven that is not of this earth, the I AM, men from having been children of God are raised to become brothers in Christ. They can ever and again draw their strength from within, as is meant by the words of Paul, "Not I but Christ in me"

The Consciousness Soul Age

The Consciousness Soul Age is the age we are in. It is still very young. By our reckoning it is less than six hundred years old and it has over a millennium and a half to go still. What this age really is, or what it is intended to become, will only be realized at the end of that time. All we can do is to characterize what we know of it up to the present. Our survey of child life from the adolescent backward was intended to help us recognize through what states of consciousness humanity has passed up to the present time but the adolescent, not yet having arrived at manhood, could not tell us where we are now. That is left to us to discover, and the age still being so young, we ourselves are little more than adolescent.

Let us then review what we know. We know that Galileo is the father of modern physics. He divided experience into two categories, what pertained to himself which came to be classed as subjective, and what, in his view, pertained to the world around him and which came to be regarded as objective. All he could rely on in his objective view of the world was what he could determine by measurement. His view of the world in terms of weight, measure, number, motion, has been adopted and developed to give us the science of technology as we know it. Today there is a machine probing planetary space at many millions of miles remove accurately controlled from the earth. At the same time this earth is being subjected to pollution of soil and water and air and has become the receptacle of deadly poisonous fallout of wastes which have to be buried in special containers for the earth itself cannot cope with it. This is one glimpse of the consciousness soul age and it indicates something totally new in the history of the world.

Contemporary with Galileo was Descartes, considered the father of modern philosophy. He set out to determine what he knew that was not derived from other sources but was really his own. This cost him years of tireless research into the contents of his own mind, and led him to a remarkable conclusion. Socrates took as his starting point, "I know that I know nothing". Descartes came to the conclusion, "I doubt". But how could he doubt if he did not think. This question led him to the further conclusion: "I doubt therefore I think". But then, how could he think if he were not there to think, hence his further step: "I doubt therefore I think therefore I am". In philosophical terms he had to confirm his own existence in this circuitous manner beginning with doubt. Unfortunately this has been generally abbreviated to "I think therefore I am". But actually all other considerations are based on the initial circumstance of doubt. This element of doubt has spread through the world so that humanity today is plunged into doubts of every kind. Most powerfully working to disrupt life is doubt of one another. We have reached a stage where, whether at government levels or in private life, doubt plays in everywhere. Rudolf Steiner questions the validity of the conclusion, "I think therefore I am". He poses the question, "Do I cease to exist when I do not think, for example, when I am asleep?" and reverses the statement to "I am therefore I think". That leaves open the question of where I am, in what realm and in what state of consciousness when I am asleep? Is it possible to enter consciously into the life of sleep? Is it possible to bring the life of sleep into the waking day?

Many questions and possibilities arise in this way which can be pursued actively. The alternative is the one followed by the behaviourists deriving the conscious faculties from bodily processes alone and leading to the conclusion that "the autonomous man" is a fiction, that the whole idea that I am something in myself is an illusion. Even if not everybody subscribes to this conclusion, we live in a world where the individual is easily and frequently brushed aside and man is treated as a thing, even as a doubtful commodity. Descartes and some of his contemporaries came to the view that the animal was no more than a kind of machine. They practised vivisection and persuaded themselves that the agonized cries of the animals could be compared to the creaking of a machine. There is factual evidence that this really happened.

That man could arrive at such a view is new and has to be regarded as a product of the consciousness soul age.

Let us turn our attention to a different kind of evidence of our modern time. Shakespeare's Hamlet has been regarded as representative of the consciousness soul man. We can dwell on a few points only.

Hamlet loved his father, loved his mother, loved Ophelia.

His 'prophetic heart' tells him that something is amiss in regard to his father's death. The Ghost, already seen by others, merely confirms what in his heart he knew already. The treachery of a brother's perfidy stands clearly before him. This question of the blood turned treacherous is a theme that Shakespeare returns to many times. This in itself shows that the world once built on the loyalty of the blood is no more, and it raises the question: what is to take its place? Then his vision of his mother, in so quickly abandoning the love and loyalty to his father to join the uncle – that vision and the trust he had in her is shattered. "Frailty, thy name is woman." This judgement then he turns upon Ophelia. Why does she return his gifts? What connivance may have brought that about? He does not trust her father, Polonius, but how can he trust her? His head out of doubt rejects her, though his heart yearns for her. Only at the end, jumping into her open grave, he declares for the whole world to hear,

> I loved Ophelia; forty thousand brothers
> Could not, with all their quantity of love,
> Make up my sum.

So in Hamlet we see how head and heart are wrenched apart, head doubts heart and heart doubts head. Our thoughts and feelings no longer go together and so action and will are also defeated.

Hamlet could so easily have ended his life with 'a bare bodkin' but the thought of what there might be beyond death, "puzzles the will" and resolute action is paralysed by "the pale cast of thought".

How widely, today, is this same puzzlement felt? Again he could so easily have killed his perfidious uncle – revenge in the old style could not satisfy his soul. It could not restore the world that has been lost.

What is left him but to use the word as a sword. His biggest deed in the play is his attempt to waken the conscience of his mother –

> O Hamlet, speak no more;
> Thou turn'st mine eyes into my very soul,

and again,

> O, speak to me no more;
> These words like daggers enter in mine ears;

But then, the Ghost intervenes,

> Oh, step between her and her fighting soul;

What manner of ghost is this? Can a ghost have compassion for the living, and, moreover, for one who, in the eyes of Hamlet, has wronged him?

Compare the Hamlet situation to that of Orestes or any other of the great Greek tragedies, and we realize that in this modern age we have entered into a totally new relationship with life, a situation which, in regard to the soul of man, is new. An earlier character, Jaques, declares, "All the world's a stage." The stage at the end of Hamlet is littered with the dead. The stage of the world today is littered with the dead, more and more each day; and everywhere, what are or could be the potentials of love destroy one another.

And now we must turn to another view of this consciousness soul age as it meets us at this very time. A cursory view sees a world full of machinery of every kind and new devices being discovered every day, a world piling up armaments of terrible might, a world that is flooded with words, in countless daily journals, weekly magazines, numberless books being poured out, radio and television unceasing as they follow the sun round, the raucous voice of humans shouting, inciting, clamouring, and wars and threats of wars going on all the time. The world has never been so noisy.

Let us look back one hundred years and what shall we see disappear? Outer space explorations and the whole of aeronautics – not a plane to be seen in the skies – maybe as a rarity an experimental balloon; no radio, radar, television; no cinemas even, and maybe the first beginning of an automobile creeping into view. A silent world, the torrents of words cease – but for the few – a world of illiterates. No question of atomic power, of nuclear threats, Einstein's formula did not exist as yet, though radioactivity was being explored and the electron had been discovered. Now let us look back two hundred years, electric power, steam power, vanish from the scene and therefore also locomotives and steamships. The hum of industry is silenced for no steam engine had yet been invented. James Watt developed his steam pump in 1765. What will be left? Nature, a stage coach on the road, a sailing ship on the water, and, alas, gunpowder still on the battlefields. Only two hundred years ago.

Now reverse the process – from the steam pump, to the steam engine and the rise of new industrial populations, to the locomotives (George Stephenson's Rocket won the prize in 1829) and steamships. Faraday was at work. Already in the thirties he was discovering the laws of electro-magnetism which presently gave rise to the dynamo, electric light and electric power available across big distances, and the harnessing of watersheds. And then the discovery and the release of atomic energy. Modern traffic is multiplying in quantity and speed, so that today there is already concern about energy resources, coal and oil will be exhausted in the not very distant future. And not to be overlooked, the triumphs of chemistry advancing rapidly to replace natural products with synthetic ones.

But most of all the horrors that might be released at any time to bring about holocausts and devastation on an unimaginable scale. This stupendous change where all the world is interlocked as one and yet has never been more divided – what then will the picture be in two hundred years' time from now? The mind reels at the thought as we see civilization of today hanging on the edge of an abyss down which it might be hurtling at any moment.

This amazing spectacle of accelerating 'progress', if that is what it is to be called, must have a ground source for its beginning in the world process of development, but here we need the longer view that only spiritual science can give. There are two approaches which we can best follow. The following sketch may help to elucidate one of them.

Post-Atlantean epoch	Stage of Earth development	Cosmic background
Ancient Indian epoch	Polaria	Ancient Saturn
Ancient Persian epoch	Hyperborea	Ancient Sun
Ancient Egyptian epoch	Lemuria	Ancient Moon
Graeco–Roman epoch	Atlantis mid-stage of the present Earth	—
The Modern epoch	—	—

Ancient Indian culture was a repetition in terms of human experience of what had ruled as divine creative process in Polaria which in itself, as the first stage in the present Earth evolution, was a recapitulation of Ancient Saturn. So, too, with regard to Ancient Persia in relation to Hyperborea, the second stage of the Earth as a recapitulation of the Ancient Sun. So, too, in relation to the Ancient Egyptian epoch, Lemuria and the Ancient Moon. Graeco-Roman culture relates through Atlantis to the middle stage of the Earth.

The fifth Post-Atlantean epoch is not a recapitulation of the past in a similar way. It has no such past. It marks, in the whole of cosmic–earthly evolution, a new starting point towards a state of the world as yet unborn.

Contained in this fact is the greatest secret of the present time and its most significant feature, the break with authority, with ruling traditions and orthodoxies and the ever-repeated demands for freedom, emancipation, self-determination. However they may have been misrepresented at times, freedom and emancipation take supremacy over all other calls and demands in this consciousness soul age since the fifteenth century.

For two thousand years Aristotle was held the supreme authority in science, then came Galileo who rejected and displaced him. The Catholic Church held unquestioned authority based on apostolic succession from the time of Peter. Then came Luther pinning up his Declaration of Independence and the Reformation had arrived. Along with this came the translation of the Bible into the vernacular, so that the Holy Word became available to all. There came political emancipation from royalty; in France with all the violence of the French Revolution, in England through the civil war between the Royalists and the Roundheads. The Royalists with their cry of the divine right of kings, the Roundheads pointing to their cropped heads as the only testimony they would abide by. There then followed, politically, the idea of democracy, ideally giving to each one his share in the government of the country. We recall the American fathers seeking freedom of worship in another land – Thanksgiving Day is still nationally celebrated; and later the American Declaration of Independence. There came the battle for the emancipation of slaves. In this century began the emancipation of women from their age-old dependence on men. One could go on extending this list, for the struggle for freedom and self-determination continues to this day, on how many fronts?

Freedom in the past meant freedom from outer bondage and compulsion. Today it has acquired a further meaning, a finding of oneself, a birth from within. At the time of the French Revolution there were many who believed that humanity was about to enter into a new age of freedom. They were soon to be disillusioned. The freedom they dreamed of was to be sought elsewhere. Coleridge was one

of the many to suffer disappointment. It was just this that
led him to write the following words:

> . . . on that sea-cliff's verge
> Where pines, scarce travelled by the breeze above
> Had made one murmur with the distant surge,
> Yes, while I stood and gazed with temples bare,
> And shot my being through earth, sea and air,
> Possessing all things with intensest love,
> O Liberty! my spirit felt thee there.

In these words Coleridge has uttered something that
speaks for the inmost character of the Consciousness Soul
age, freedom born of the spirit out of love for all creation.
This same experience is the crowning one of Shelley's
Prometheus Unbound – only love for the world can free
Prometheus from the rock to which he is bound. This is also
the triumphant chorus that ends Beethoven's ninth symphony. It is in the world, it lives in men, yet remains
a far-off ideal, whereas in life as we meet it, all seems
confusion and contradiction. Why is this?

Here we need again to turn to spiritual science for a longer
and larger view seen historically, to elucidate the dilemma
in which man finds himself. Longing and, as he believes,
striving ardently for freedom, he finds himself caught
increasingly in conditions or threats of unfreedom.

The question arises at what point in this whole evolution
does man himself, as conscious ego, enter into the process
to play his responsible part. It cannot be while his sheaths
are being prepared, his physical body, etheric body, astral
body – that can only be the work of the gods. It can only be
in the course of the post-Atlantean epochs as the life of
thought develops and man advances in self-awareness. By
the end of Atlantis man has been brought so far forward in
his physical body that he can walk in an upright position,
that his larynx is so far formed that he can utter speech, and
that his brain, too, has reached a stage that makes possible

the lighting up of thought, but all this as a very elementary beginning. In all regards, man is still utterly and completely dependent on guidance from without, that is, from high initiation sources. And now we learn that in the first Post-Atlantean epoch, the task of the Seven Holy Rishis was to bring down the forces for shaping and perfecting the etheric body; the caste system, as we have described it, is an expression of this. So, too, the mighty task of Zarathustra was to bring order and organization into the astral body. Only then does the human ego which has been resting in and with the gods begin its descent into the three sheaths.

As the ego works upon the sheaths, so an interiorized life of soul begins for man. Egyptian culture is the expression of the work of the ego upon the astral body, awakening the first stage of personalized consciousness as sentient soul. Astrology, or the reading of human destiny from the stars, is one aspect of the dawning sense of selfhood. Graeco-Roman culture came about through the working of the ego-forces upon the etheric body thus giving rise to the mind soul or intellectual soul, hence the birth of philosophy marking a stronger degree of interiorized experience and self-identity. This continued through the Middle Ages. We have only to think of such an outstanding figure as Thomas Aquinas. Then from early in the fifteenth century the ego descended into the physical body providing the basis for the strongly accentuated sense of selfhood of today with the birth of the consciousness soul. Thus the three last culture epochs show the progression from sentient-soul to intellectual-soul to consciousness-soul. As we have seen also in considering Kali-yuga, this process of entering into the bodies meant, on the one hand a heightening of the personality sense, and on the other, the fading away of a natural awareness of the spirit at work in nature. The Egyptians with their sentient-soul still retained a live relationship to the world of the stars. The Greeks in their thinking still experienced the life-creating forces in the world. We in our age have lost all that. We have built up a world-conception seeking by logic to interpret observation confined to the outer appearance of phenomena. But this logic which we have inherited from the Greeks has lost its inner grasp of existence and turned into mere abstractionism.

It is in the Graeco-Roman epoch that Christ made his final descent to the earth for, as we have also seen, he was ever the guiding divinity, the bearer and upholder of the law, ruling and directing human progress. At this time Christ descended to earth, to confirm by his own deed of incarnation as man, the establishment of ego incarnation for mankind. Amongst those who were living at that time, a time when men were not as body-bound as we are, there were some, the disciples and others, who became his followers. They apprehended the divinity that enveloped and penetrated the being of Jesus, though it completely surpassed their understanding. Only by slow degrees could they awaken somewhat to the mystery of the being in whose presence they lived and moved. What Christ achieved through his incarnation is to lead to the spiritualization and the passing away of the world through the mediation of evolving humanity. In that mystery we still live and move, for the most part unknowingly.

Under ordinary conditions today, the ego is so deeply incarnated into the physical body that man finds himself in his consciousness at the boundary of the senses, as though arrested there. If he looks inwards, his intellectual mind reveals nothing to him of his essential being. If he gazes through his senses outwards he finds himself a stranger to the world around him. If he attempts to draw back into himself he grows lost to the world. If he identifies himself with the outer physical world he grows lost to himself. Either way he seems condemned to a life of loneliness and unfulfilment. Inner and outer do not meet. Thus, in his soul he lapses into a state of desolation, emptiness, unrelatedness. We think of T. S. Eliot's "hollow men".

The condition of Marlowe's Faustus typifies much of present day man. Unable to solve the riddle of his own being in the world around him, he all too easily becomes a devotee of Lucifer who would lead him off into realms of mystical fantasy; or he falls a prey to the machinations of Ahriman who, with utmost cunning, infiltrates into his thinking to persuade him that the world is no more than a machine and he a replaceable part in it.

This is the dangerous time in which we are living. Whether through illusory idealism or delusory realism, man grows divorced from the source of his own being in the Logos, in Christ. He denies his own true egohood to himself. The impulse to explore, discover and create anew proceeds from the Ego he is so apt to forget or ignore. The impulse which launched the scientific adventure and along with it the search for freedom proceeds from the very nature of his I AM. But life today is spread to the bounds of the physical and man is as though trapped within these bounds.

Anthroposophy builds on the two faculties of observation and thinking. Strengthened thinking through inner exercise and freedom from preconceived theory in observing can lead, beyond the peripheric limits of the physical, to an enhanced consciousness that transcends what are today regarded as the limits of knowledge, both in regard to the world outside and the life within. Then we begin to awaken also to the workings of Lucifer and Ahriman, to the parts they play in the world and therefore also in us. We cannot merely flee from them but we can learn to direct to human ends the forces they exert.

Then the term consciousness-soul can acquire a new name, spiritual-soul. We have not yet awakened in the spirit but we have awakened to it. Life takes on a new character and human endeavour a new direction. We begin to see more clearly why we cannot live any longer by drawing wisdom from the past, necessary as this may be for the understanding of the present, but we are called on to shape a future out of the intuitive powers of the will. Here, humanity without the Christ-ened ego to help, is in great danger of losing its way between Lucifer the tempter, and Ahriman the deceiver.

Consciousness-soul or spiritual-soul means to recognize the situation of present-day man in full consciousness, to awaken to the particular dangers and temptations which this age offers, and to know what measures need to be taken to meet them, measures to be born as free initiatives.

Re-incarnation and Individual Destiny

The teaching of re-incarnation has lived in the East from ancient times and was renewed and reformed by Buddha in the sixth century BC. It never found a place in Christian tradition. Now, today, we find it brought forward with a different emphasis in anthroposophy. It is these three conditions we wish to consider.

Buddha stands as the great teacher of compassion. It was out of his compassion that he brought his teachings. He saw earth existence as steeped in pain and grief. Birth is suffering, age is suffering, sickness is suffering, death is suffering; but also being separated from those we love is suffering, being compelled to live with what we do not love is suffering, being unable to fulfill one's desires is suffering. The cause of these ills he attributed to the lust, the craving for sensely living, which possessed the soul. The only way to overcome this was through exercising wise restraint in all respects and cultivating a meditative life. Only this could lead to the peace and tranquillity whereby the soul could be made free of the bondage of repeated lives on earth. Buddha, having overcome temptation and achieved illumination knew that never again would he himself have to live in an earthly body. Out of his own experiences he brought forward the Eightfold Path, whereby every soul that persevered could gain similar release and win the way to

Nirvana, the land of bliss and blessedness. It is a striving to reattain the primordial virtues from which life on earth has fallen away.

The Path is expressed very simply in words and made accessible to everyone. It can be briefly expressed as follows:

Right understanding and right aspiring in contemplating life;

Right speech, right conduct, and right vocation in the daily dealing with life;

Right effort, right awakeness, right concentration in transcending the hold of life.

This, in broad terms, is Dharma, the way of Truth.

The Christian emphasis has always been on life in the present – not Christ WAS, but Christ IS.

"The Kingdom of Heaven is at hand", said John the Baptist, to which Christ added, "My Kingdom is not of this world". Henceforth man, looking into himself, may come to learn that the central core of his being, his I AM, belongs to the Kingdom whence Christ descended. "And the Word became flesh and dwelt among us." The Word which was from the beginning, had entered the stream of earthly human evolution. "Heaven and earth will pass away but my word will not pass away."

Therefore man's task is in this world, the world in which all things have been bound for man's sake, in which all that has been bound is waiting to be unbound. In the words of Paul, "All nature groaneth and travaileth waiting upon the redemption of man". Human progress and world progress are one; the words, "I am with you always", can be understood to have been spoken for all mankind, for the living as well as the dead who, in their sphere, have their tasks also.

What is determinative is that everything is to happen in the ever-renewing present. It thus came about that the holiest striving in the Christian centuries was to walk in the footsteps of Christ, and, in esoteric terms, to meditate on the stages of the Passion: The washing of the feet; the flagellation; the crowning with thorns; the crucifixion; the death on the cross; the resurrection and the ascension. Christ's last words at parting as given in the Acts are as follows: "And he said unto them, It is not for you to know the times and the seasons, which the Father hath put in his own power. But you shall receive power, after that the Holy Ghost shall come upon you; and ye shall witness unto me both in Jerusalem, and in Samaria, and unto the uttermost part of the earth."

The Word is for all men. Ten days later came Pentecost and the descent of the Holy Ghost, the Holy Spirit, upon the disciples as they sat gathered in an 'upper room'. They were to convey what they had received to all mankind, to each one in his own tongue, which can also mean in the measure of his understanding.

That which Christ brought is the ever-recurring living in the present. "I am in the Father, and ye in me, and I in you". The words "Even as ye have done it unto the least of my brethren, ye have done it unto me," are as true this very day as ever they were then. With the emphasis on the NOW, the teaching of reincarnation vanished from view.

"By this shall all men know that ye are my disciples, if ye have love for one another".

We live in a mystery that is unending. Hence the closing words of the Gospel of St John of which Rudolf Steiner made special mention.

"And there are many other things that Jesus did, the which if they should be written every one, I suppose that even the world itself could not contain the books that should be written. Amen".

Entry into the Consciousness Soul epoch has brought humanity to a totally new evolutionary stage. The direction of life has swung strongly towards the future. It is an age where will is uppermost. We have seen this in the release of steam power, electric power, and now nuclear power, rapidly transforming the face of the earth. Man has to come to terms with himself as never before. He has to achieve a great moral-spiritual advance or see himself overwhelmed within and without by the powers which, almost unwittingly, he has himself released. This situation has assumed gravest proportions, precisely in the twentieth century, since the end of Kali-yuga. There is a veritable struggle going forward between the force of the awakening spirit and the materialistic powers that are ranged against it.

The knowledge of re-incarnation, which may come newly to us through anthroposophy, should play a considerable role in securing human balance. Born of an understanding of man which ranges beyond the limitations of birth and death, it opens up new vistas for the future.

Let us return to the view of man in his threefold nature of thinking, feeling and willing. With his thinking man is enabled to survey the past. He can bring the fruits of the past to have bearing on the present. What he cannot do with his thinking is to project himself into an actual future – he may have surmises, hopes and expectations, but that is all. With his will the opposite is the case. He can initiate deeds in the present for fulfilment in the future. What he cannot do with his will is to make a re-entry into the past – he cannot will backwards. With his feeling he can strike the balance between the evidences of the past and the intentions for the future and hope to arrive at present judgement.

These considerations we can carry further. With every outgoing thought, feeling, word or deed we place the impress of our being upon the world around us. Something has parted from us to find a place in the world. This, however, works back equally upon ourselves, setting its mark in us.

Rudolf Steiner once illustrated the nature of destiny (or karma) in the image of a bow and arrow. The arrow leaves the bow with a certain force, but in the same measure produces a recoil in the bow. In life we are the bow, and our thoughts and feelings and actions are the arrows we send forthwith into the world around, but we bear the recoil in ourselves.

Now a stage further. At the end of the day we retire to sleep. When we waken in the morning we are not in the same condition as the night before. Something transpires between sleeping and waking. How we have lived in the day, being inscribed in us, we meet in the night. Sleep brings change. In the alternations of day and night something is achieved which we may observe and life builds up accordingly. Our observation and judgement during the night of the day that has passed is completely objective and this works objectively in us, whereby we grow.

This then is how individual destiny works from day to day, to be seen in its results. Whatever other powers may come to meet us in the night to renew health and strength for the morrow, by what we do, or fail to do, and by our manner of doing, we are still the prime arbiters of our individual destinies.

Along this way of thinking we come to see how justifiably sleep has been likened to a younger brother of death. In death we leave the world behind us with all we have impressed upon it. Inevitably we carry the counterpart of this with us through death. But what we have left behind is every bit as much a part of us, as what we bear away. The one belongs to the other, and as Egos we are equally involved in both.

If day and night are absolute conditions of our daily life, so that day is unthinkable without night or night without day, why should that be less so in the longer range as between life and death. We are not born in the morning out of a state of nothingness but out of the day before; we bring with us a preparedness for the new day. So, too, we may consider that we enter the world through birth uniquely equipped in our different ways for a new life. Where could we have gathered this equipment other than through a life or many lives before. To attribute all this to an ad hoc adjustment of inherited genes may seem an easy thought, but it leaves too much out of account. A human being in his ego, or I AM, carries a singleness which is indivisible, as distinct from a personality composed of many parts.

It is our own self we meet in the world in the impress we have laid upon it. It is our own destiny we meet in those we have met before, to carry our mutual adventure further. In the vast complex of human relationships we may learn to know ourselves responsible to one another, each to all and all to each. Looked squarely in the face, it cannot be otherwise. Where and when and at what point we meet one another, at what ages, older or younger, ceases to be casual and takes on a depth of meaning. We make room in our lives for one another. In this new age we also make room for the gods to re-enter, so that the story of man and the world begins once again to assume an epic grandeur. Should there be some who say, "But this is mere makebelief," we can only reply, "God bless the makebelief" since it endows our relationships with a greater, more meaningful reality. But truth needs no apologist, it proves itself. Experience adds to experience and evidence to evidence if we but choose to be attentive. Every individual advance is a gift to the whole community, every failure or shortcoming a loss to all, – so closely knit are our lives together. The totality of existence will not permit of anybody being left out or cast aside.

The study of re-incarnation in the form now given is not based on credence. It opens up a great field for study and exploration. It carries human encounters into many life-times. That few, at the present time, recall their past lives can only be accounted a blessing, for in this realm, we are warned, there can be countless illusions unless the soul is sufficiently purified and freed from all self-love.

There is for many a will to return to the earth, a will to

meet one another here on earth out of the kingdom that is not of the earth, in order to fulfil the needs of the earth; that Christ's deeds for man and the world shall not have been in vain. Then the words, "Where two or three are gathered in my name, there am I also," become a seed of promise that can multiply to include in course of time the whole of humanity.

In earlier times it was communities born out of inherited pasts that sustained the individuals composing them. From now on and into the future, in this age of light which we have entered, it will be individual human beings who, out of their moral independence and inner freedom, will create and sustain new communities in the spirit.

The future rests on the free-born deeds of men and women who have learnt to know one another in the spirit. We are moving into a future when the vicarious deed of Christ for all mankind will become the archetype of human deeds for one another. Then we will know that Christ moves amongst us, the guiding Lord of human destiny.

It will be seen that no one can offer fruit to another, unless he has laboured and brought forth that fruit. It lives as a newly arising conscience in modern·men to labour and bring forth fruit for one another. May He who named Himself, "I am the I am", and whom we have learned to name the Christ, be with us in our mutual labours.

Towards the Future

The Confrontation with Death

WE BEGIN TO SEE, with the help of anthroposophy, that the story of man, far from being the mindless process of chance and probability of modern science, involves all the hierarchies known to antiquity and the early church reaching up to the Holy Trinity as well as the opposition forces which derive from these same hierarchies. One direct consequence of that opposition is the phenomenon of death following on the fall.

It is to be noted that Genesis has two distinct accounts of the creation. The first one proceeds from day to day, in all tranquillity. When everything else had been prepared, then God said, "Let us make man in our own image . . . in the image of God created he him; male and female created he them". Then came the seventh day on which "God ended his work" and that was the day of rest.

> And God blessed the seventh day, and sanctified it: because that in it he had rested from all his work which God created and made.

There is no hint of anything adverse, of a temptation and a fall. This whole account suggests creation from Ancient Saturn and Ancient Sun up to the end and conclusion of Ancient Moon, by which time the creation of man was already indicated, hence the second version begins with "the generations of the heavens and the earth when they were first created". Then, very soon there is mention of the creation of man: "And the Lord God formed man of the dust of the ground, and breathed into his nostrils the breath of life; and man became a living soul." There follows, immediately after, the creation of the Garden of Eden . . . "the tree of life also in the midst of the garden, and the tree of knowledge of good and evil."

Next God put the man into the garden to tend it – only plants have been mentioned so far. Then comes mention of 'the man' being alone. "I will make him an help meet for him." But before that happens the Lord God formed every beast of the field and every fowl of the air, and brought them to Adam, having now received his own name, to be named by him. Adam was thus raised above all the new creation up to that time, with a consciousness superior to all the beasts. Only then did God cause "a deep sleep to fall upon Adam, and he slept". And from the side of Adam, as an extension of his being, did he create a woman . . . "and they shall be one flesh". It is stated that "they were both naked, the man and his wife, and were not ashamed". They were in a state of paradisal bliss, with a consciousness that rested wholly in God. The trees of knowledge of good and evil and of life had already been shown to Adam before the creation of Eve, with a warning about the former, not to eat of it, "for in the day that thou eatest thereof thou shalt surely die"; not that they were never to eat of it, but they were not yet mature enough to do so. No similar warning is given about the tree of life.

Then came the serpent "more subtil than any beast of the field" to tempt the woman. She quoted Adam as having been warned of God, "Ye shall not eat of it, neither shall ye touch it lest ye die." Now, as yet, there had been no death in the world. The serpent, therefore, could have known nothing about death. He assures her that God will not have her die. "Your eyes shall be opened, and ye shall be as gods, knowing good and evil." They were jumped through Lucifer into a consciousness for which they were not ready. They were filled with apprehension and beheld each other with new eyes. They were thrust into a different condition of life. The eyes that had beheld God could no longer see. The eyes they now possessed were to lead to an outer seeing but remained blind to God.

This second story Rudolf Steiner places in Lemuria which recapitulates the Ancient Moon. Just as the human being, towards the end of Lemuria, was emerging to his own true shape in uprightness before God, came Lucifer, previously fallen from his own high estate, to insinuate himself into the soul of man. Being of a supersensible nature, he sought a domain in the supersensible nature of the human being who was thus through him first brought to confusion and grief.

Henceforth man, in the words of Faust, carried two souls within his breast; he became a divided nature, more deeply sunk in matter than he should have been, thus blinded in soul and maimed in body, leading to death. The Bible tells that God made "coats of skins and clothed them" and he said, "Behold the man has become one of us to know good and evil" but they were cast out of Eden lest Adam "should put forth his hand and take also of the tree of life, and eat, and live for ever". Henceforth death must be their portion, but then, also, the overcoming of death by the deed of a God in compensation for the deed of a God, that separation through death might be overcome by the power of love, and freedom be born and the mission of the Earth be fulfilled as "Love in Freedom".

Christ's deed in entering the stream of human destiny, in suffering death with man, was to plant in man the seed of immortality, whereby each one, uniting himself with the Christ deed, might find the forces ultimately to overcome Lucifer himself, and conquer the death forces that assail his soul.

We may ask, why Christ did not come at the midpoint of Atlantis which was the actual midpoint of the whole earth evolution. Rudolf Steiner explains that owing to the displacement of the bodies through the deed of Lucifer, Christ waited for a period as long after that midpoint as the one from the temptation to that midpoint. Hence he descended to Earth during the fourth post-Atlantean epoch.

Christ, after the resurrection, was able to teach the disciples as no other God has taught before or since for he alone of all supersensible beings had suffered death. He laid into them a seed for all future times until the passing away of the world. At the end of that forty days, on the day of the Ascension, as his parting words before he was to vanish from their view, he said that the Holy Spirit would come upon them and with the power it would bring them, they were to bear witness of what they had experienced "unto the uttermost part of the earth".

There is still the confrontation with Ahriman to be considered. When Adam and Eve, through Lucifer, were cast out of Paradise, when the light in which they had lived in Paradise was extinguished in their souls, they found themselves in an outer world that was cold and dark and breathed of death, the domain of Ahriman. Christ had overcome him for the sake of man, but the battle to be waged by man himself still lay ahead. For that we turn to the Book of Revelation. The tremendous imaginations in this book bear the character of prophetic visions regarding the further destiny of man.

"And there appeared a great wonder in heaven; a woman clothed with the sun, and the moon under her feet, and upon her head a crown of twelve stars."

Thus a figure of cosmic dimensions.

"And she being with child cried, travailing in birth, and pained to be delivered."

There is then described "a great red dragon" whose "tail drew the third part of the stars of heaven."

The dragon stood before the woman ready "to devour her child as soon as it was born".

"And she brought forth a man child" who was caught up unto God, and to his throne.

There is then described a mighty war in heaven, in which

Michael and his angels fought the dragon and his angels. And the dragon and his host were cast out of heaven and down upon the earth.

Who was the man-child who was newly born – who but the true ego in man, the I AM – that was "to rule all nations with a rod of iron" – iron as an image of the purified will that rules in the blood, won for man "by the blood of the Lamb".

But then the words follow: "Woe to the inhabiters of the earth and of the sea! for the devil is come down unto you, having great wrath, because he knoweth that he hath but a short time."

Thus the war that was fought and won in heaven is now descended to be continued by the human beings now on earth.

We recall that Lucifer slipped into the unsuspecting soul when it was still in its earliest infancy, that even at the end of Atlantis the consciousness in man could be compared to a child of three saying 'I' for the first time. And we have followed how that selfhood awareness has strengthened from epoch to epoch. Even all through the fourth epoch, the human soul was still under protection. It is only in the present age, in the age of the consciousness-spiritual soul that the human ego has begun really to come into its own as a conscious and independent individuality, as the 'man-child', to usher in the age of freedom. The above description in the Book of Revelation, whatever other truths it may contain, most certainly has relevance for the time we are in. We are daily engaged in a battle for the freedom of the human spirit against powers that would quell that freedom. We live in an age in which death has grown rampant. We meet it in forms that would subjugate soul and spirit, not to speak of the threats of physical annihilation. We need to know the dragon before we meet him. But we need also to know that he has been overcome in higher realms and that this is the age, if ever there was one, in which humanity is being tested to the full. Wars, greater and lesser, are breaking out everywhere, and these must continue until the inner battle in the spirit has prevailed. The further act of that great drama rests on man. Anthroposophy has come at this much needed time to awaken, to nourish, and to fortify the spirit of man.

This Michael Age

Michael today is little more than a legendary figure even though there is a day in the calendar, September 29th, dedicated to him. And to speak of a Michael Age is well-nigh incomprehensible to most people. Yet anthroposophy has much to say about him, the archangel who was ever closest to Christ in his service to man. Indeed, anthroposophy in the form in which we have received it comes as Michael's awakening call, "Man, know thyself!", evolved by Rudolf Steiner into a spiritual language for today.

The following Celtic verse shows how strongly Michael still lived in the imagination of the people not so very long ago.

> Thou Michael the Victorious,
> I make my circuit under thy shield.
> Thou Michael of the white steed
> And of the bright, brilliant blade,
> Conqueror of the dragon
> Be thou at my back.
> Thou ranger of the heavens,
> Thou warrior of the King of All,
> Thou Michael the Victorious,
> My pride and my guide,
> Thou Michael the Victorious,
> The glory of mine eye.

A peasant, at the end of his day's labour in the field, gazing into the sunset, might well pray to Michael to carry him under his wings to the throne of God. So warmly did

Michael live in the hearts of simple folk.

We learn that Michael inspired Alexander the Great, the pupil of Aristotle, on his great journeys to establish centres for rekindling and renewing the mystery wisdom, otherwise dying out, in preparation for the coming of Christ.[1]

Michael, we learn, was the guiding spirit of the Arthurian mysteries which date back in origin to several centuries B C. The Knights of the Round Table formed a spiritual community in the service of the Cosmic Christ, the Sun-Logos, the Sun-Hero, the King of the Elements working in nature. They could therefore be called pre-Christian Christians, though the Fellowship did continue also into the early Christian centuries.

Michael was equally the guiding spirit of the Grail Mysteries in the guardianship of the Templar Knights.

The Arthurian Fellowship broke up by disruption from within, the Grail Fellowship by destruction from without. In both instances the dragon appeared to prevail. Indeed, the battle with the dragon is a recurring one at every stage of human history where a forward step is to be taken. Then the adversary powers we have described gather up to their fullest strength, a historic crisis ensues, and the battle is renewed. We are involved in a gathering crisis at this time as wide-ranging as the world and, as regards man's share in it, unprecedented.

First, since we have shown that the archangel Michael is active always, what makes particularly a *Michael age*? Secondly, what is the particular form of the Dragon at this time?

We learn how each culture epoch has a prevailing character under the suzerainty of an Archai or Spirit of Personality. We learn further that such an epoch is divided into seven sub-periods of about three hundred and fifty years, each such sub-period in the care of a particular Archangel.

[1]*Cosmic Christianity and the Impulse of Michael.* Lecture series. Torquay 1924.

There are seven such Archangels who take charge in rotation. During the allotted time, each of these Archangels is able to unfold his special gifts within the all-ruling character established by the Archai. Michael is such an Archangel and from the year 1879 he has taken over the leadership, so that everything we can call Michaelic has an opportunity at the present time of influencing human life most profoundly. To this we will return.

And now with regard to the dragon, we see him in a two-fold character, bitterly divided yet single in purpose to undermine the cosmic plan for man. This two-foldness is expressed in the figures of Lucifer and Ahriman. In the mediaeval picture of the dragon we see him belching forth fire and fury from the belly whilst outwardly ensheathed in a mail of icy deathly coldness; unrestrained passion and unmitigated hate. There are times when it is Lucifer who appears to predominate in which case Mephistopheles or Ahriman acts as servitor, and at other times the reverse is the case. In Faustus we saw Mephistopheles with his cold and calculating cunning as the active agent; there comes a moment when he calls in his Lord Lucifer. Both have their parts to play. Today, and ever since the dawn of a science divorced from man, it is clearly Ahriman who is everywhere dominant; he is now the Lord, with Lucifer acting a secondary rôle. The cold hate of Ahriman is a passion which seizes people and proliferates conscience-less cruelty and destruction; and the wiles of Lucifer to lull the soul through all manner of self-indulgences and distractions carry a deadly sting in them. Today gives ample evidence of both.

In Raphael's painting of St George and the dragon we see in the distance the figure of a young woman kneeling in prayer and supplication that she be not devoured by the Dragon. This kneeling figure represents the human soul. Very different is the picture in the Book of Revelation where Satan rises up to devour the man-child the moment it is born. The man-child is the human spirit, the I AM, whose arrival has been long prepared for and now the moment has come. Ahriman wishes to destroy conscious egohood that no being shall arrive to rule with a rod of iron – iron as human will. His aim is to produce a race of spirit-less, will-less beings – 'hollow men'.

How may we interpret the picture in the Book of Revelation in terms of today?

To answer this we have to open up an aspect of the working of the archangel Michael which, so far, only anthroposophy has been able to reveal, namely, his relationship to the life of thought. The Celtic verse we have quoted describes Michael as "ranger of the heavens". Anthroposophy or spiritual science describes him as the Ruler of Cosmic Intelligence. All the heavenly bodies are directed in their motions and changing relationships by divine intelligences. All this weaving, working, inter-relating of multiple intelligences, it was the task of Michael to co-ordinate into an integrated whole and to convey it to mankind on earth. In the past, even after the birth of Greek philosophy, there had not yet arisen the feeling of 'I think', but rather 'a God thinks in me'. A thought was something borne towards one by an angel being or divine messenger. Such thoughts then came as divinely given.

And here comes the great mystery. Even as Christ inclined himself more and more towards mankind until he placed his being totally into human hands, so, ever faithful to Christ, Michael allowed his rulership of the World Intelligence to pass to man. From about the ninth century AD men began, more and more, to experience thoughts as arising from within themselves, less and less as derived from a higher source, until, with the birth of the consciousness soul, with the immersion of the human spirit in the physical body, there awoke, as we have described it, a highly accentuated sense of selfhood but at the same time a loss of conscious connection with the spirit. Man began to regard his thoughts, not even as arising from within himself, but merely as mental reflections of the physical processes around him. With his blindness to the spirit in nature, man, seeing himself as no more than a piece of nature, arrived at a thinking which not only denies the divine but also his own actual being to himself. To this type of God-voided thinking, the words of Christ, "My kingdom is not of this world" cease to have any meaning.

All this was foreseen as an unavoidable precondition for an age of freedom. But unless man can emerge from this trial in which the gods appear to have abandoned him to feel himself divorced from reality, he must with equal inevitability multiply unfreedom to the point where he is in danger of annihilating his being altogether. This danger lay ahead.

The time was approaching for the present Michael age. It was the time when, from Galileo on, the whole trend of thinking veered towards scientific materialism. On earth below, the ruling Archangel was Gabriel. In the spiritual worlds, so anthroposophy tells us, during this very time, the Archangel Michael assembled a mighty school attended by discarnate human souls and hierarchical beings. There he portrayed in mighty imaginations the history of the creation and evolution of the world and man, the mission of Christ for man from the first beginning, the place of the adversary powers in this history and much else that later formed the content of anthroposophy. This great supersensible school reached a culmination in the nineteenth century.

In the meantime the region in the heavens closest to the earth was darkened by hosts upon hosts of what are described as 'demonic idols', the dead materialistic thoughts streaming up from the earth. This was the gathering of the hosts of darkness. And there came about a war in heaven in which Michael and those who were with him fought these demon forces. Rudolf Steiner speaks of the fall of the Spirits of Darkness in the forties of the nineteenth century. They were cast out of heaven and have since been rampant on earth, achieving through men miraculous accomplishments externally, yet obliterating the vision of man and the meaning of life.

It was early in the 'sixties that Marx produced a work of genius in his *Das Kapital* but standing life on its head by making the acquisition of material resources the starting point for human progress. In the late 'fifties came Darwin's famous work, *The Origin of Species*, which presents man as the outcome of chance variations, again placing the material element as the starting point for evolution. Then came a variety of further developments, hypnotism making instincts the ground for soul experience; the materialistic interpretation of the heavens with the aid of the newly discovered spectroscope – and so on. Man, thinking himself the originator of his own thoughts, lost all conception that they might be inspired by powers inimical to his being, as Rudolf Steiner shows in *Four Mystery Dramas*.

The war in heaven became a war on earth. Rudolf Steiner was born in 1861. The New Michael Age as described by him began in 1879. He was then in his nineteenth year when he was first led to realize what his mission might be. He was to overcome the dragon by entering into him and transforming him from within. In practice he was to enter fully into the materialistic thinking of today and transform it so as to make of Natural Science a pathway to Spiritual Science. If we are to speak of the dragon today, it is Mephistopheles-Ahriman-Satan we have to deal with, by whatever name we choose to call him. His attack is on the man-child, the ego-bearer, the conscious thinker in man in this modern age.

Rudolf Steiner describes how a ray of light from the supersensible school of Michael entered the soul of Goethe, and this gave rise to his fairy tale *The Green Snake and the Beautiful Lily* in which darkness is overcome, bonds are set free, and all ends in universal rejoicing at the coming of a New Day. He describes how he felt a strong need to meditate on this work. Twenty-one years later, he wrote the first of his four mystery plays, *The Portal of Initiation*, a transformation, or better, a metamorphosis in many respects of Goethe's fairy tale. In these mystery plays we are given examples of the path of inner development as this expresses itself in a number of very different individuals. It is a path which has to find a human way between the temptations of Lucifer and the beguilement of Ahriman. The way to spiritual science opens the way to a new understanding of the Word. Inner and outer meet at a new birth stage in man, so that the consciousness soul, so deeply entered into matter, translates into the spiritual soul, a new awakening to the spirit.

This Michael Age has no precedent in that the initiative falls wholly upon man – else it could not be an age of freedom. We may say, Michael is there beside man and Christ is ever with him, but it is left to man himself to overcome, in his thinking, the Ahrimanic materialistic thinking which would dominate him. He has by his own endeavours to arrive at Michaelic truth, at a way of exploring and interpreting phenomena which transcends the abyss between self and world, and thus to overcome the moral void and inner emptiness which is bringing civilization ever more into a state of chaos. It is the opportunity for man, as never before, to assert his moral identity before God and man. As man achieves the Michaelic victory within himself, so Michael himself may hope to regain his office as regent of cosmic intelligence in marvellously new fashion through the soul of man.

How is one to work in regard to the science of today? Rudolf Steiner gives an accurate description of the way he himself worked. We have quoted something similar before, but here we have his exact wording:

. . . study the system of Haeckel with all its materialism; study it, and at the same time permeate yourselves with the methods of cognition indicated in *Knowledge of Higher Worlds and its Attainment*. Take what you learn in Haeckel's *Anthropogenesis*. In that form it may very likely repel you. Learn it nevertheless; learn all that can be learned about it by outer natural science and carry it towards the gods. You will get what is related about evolution in my *Occult Science, an Outline*. Such is the connection between the feeble, shadowy knowledge which man can acquire here, and that which the gods can give him, if with the proper spirit he duly prepares himself by the learning of this knowledge. But man must first bring towards them (i.e. the gods) what he can learn here on the Earth, for in truth the times have changed.

We carry up into a spiritual world the knowledge of nature here attained, or again, the creations of naturalistic art, or the religious sentiments working naturalistically in the soul. (Even religion has become naturalistic nowadays.) And as we carry all this upward – if we develop the necessary faculties – we do indeed encounter Michael.

Rudolf Steiner describes how in earlier times men could meet Michael as in a kind of dream, but "since the end of the last third of the nineteenth century, men can meet Michael in the Spirit, in *a fully conscious way*".

And now, how does Michael react to men's endeavours?

Michael is a being who reveals nothing if we ourselves do not bring him something from our diligent spiritual work on Earth. Michael is a silent spirit – silent and reserved. Michael is taciturn. He is a spirit who speaks very little. At most he will give sparing indications, for what we learn from Michael is not really the word, but, if I may so express it – the look, the power, the direction of his gaze.

This is because Michael concerns himself most of all with that which men *create* out of the spirit. He lives with the consequences of all that men have created. The other spirits live more with the causes: Michael lives with the consequences. The other spirits kindle in man the impulse for that which he shall do. Michael will be the true spiritual hero of freedom; he lets men do, and he then takes what becomes of human deeds, receives it, and carries it on and out into the cosmos, to continue in the cosmos what men themselves cannot yet do with it.

For other beings of the hierarchy of the Archangeloi, we feel that impulses are coming from them. Michael is the spirit from whom no impulses come to begin with; for his most characteristic epoch is the one now at hand when things are to arise out of human freedom. But when man does things out of spiritual activity, or inner freedom . . . then Michael carries the earthly deed out into the cosmos; so it becomes cosmic deed. Michael takes care for the results; the other spirits care more for the causes.

However, Michael is not only a silent, taciturn spirit. Michael meets man with a very clear gesture of repulsion for many things in which the human being of today still lives on Earth. For example, all knowledge that arises as to the life of men or animals or plants, tending to lay stress on inherited characteristics – on all that is inherited in physical nature – is such that we feel Michael constantly repelling it, driving it away with deprecation. He means to say that such knowledge cannot help man at all for the spiritual world. Only what man discovers in the human and animal and plant kingdoms independently of the purely hereditary nature, can be carried up before Michael. Then we receive, not the eloquent gesture of deprecation, but the look of approval which tells us that it is a thought righteously conceived in harmony with cosmic guidance.

He also sternly rejects all separating elements such as the

human language. So long as we only clothe our knowledge in these languages and do not carry it right up into our thoughts, we cannot come near Michael.

Among the things that would fain reject the impulse of Michael today are the feelings of nationality. They flared up in the nineteenth century and became strong in the twentieth – stronger and stronger [1924]. By the principle of nationality many things have been ordered, or rather, have become sadly disordered in the most recent times.

All this is in terrible opposition to the Michael principle; all this contains Ahrimanic forces which strive against the inpouring of the Michael force into the earthly life of man. So then we see this battle of the upward-attacking Ahrimanic spirits who would like to carry upward what comes through the inherited impulses of nationality – which Michael strongly rejects and repels.

The world must receive once more the principle of initiation as such among the principles of civilization. Only thereby will it come about that man, here on the earth, will gather in his soul something with which he can go before Michael, so as to meet Michael's approving look, the look that says: 'that is right, cosmically right.' Thereby the will is made fast and firm, and the human being is incorporated in the spiritual progress of the universe. Thereby, man himself becomes a co-operator in that which is about to be instilled into the evolution of mankind on Earth by Michael – beginning now in this present epoch of Michael.[1]

The Great Group – a Testimony

Rudolf Steiner was at one time occupied with the question: how could one portray the countenance of Christ?

The author was once given a volume of portraits of Christ. There were reproductions from many great artists.

[1] *A Michael Lecture*, Dornach 1921.

Each one, in his own inimitable way had captured something of the quality through that which lived in his own soul. Immensely different though these renderings were, they bore witness to an ideal, a source that lived in them all – each one's testimony so far as his individuality could reach.

Was it possible to go further, to conceive of a countenance that was beyond the personal and yet all-humanly human? Was not that the striving of every great artist – to surpass the personal for the all-human? Rudolf Steiner's approach to the question was remarkably unexpected. Briefly it was as follows.

The human being is held in a body which separates him from all around him. This is a fact of his destiny. Through this condition of separation he knows himself distinct from all else in the world. This condition of separation provides for three fundamental qualities of experience: wonder, compassion and conscience.

Only through our separation can we awaken wonder at the world in all its manifestations. The soul is moved to feelings of wonder. The Greeks said: 'Philosophy begins with wonder'. There is no comprehension of the world without the sense of wonder which carries us beyond the mere seeing. How sad and impoverished is the soul that is lacking in wonder.

Compassion also we can only awaken and develop through the fact of separation. Compassion means literally 'to suffer with', to enter into the sorrows and needs of another. How desolating to have no compassion in one's heart for others. We may think of Buddha and how all his teaching was born out of his compassion.

And then conscience. We have seen how conscience awoke in the *Orestes* of Euripides – he was made to confront a wrong and his conscience gave him no peace, for the wrong demanded to be righted.

Before the birth of conscience men lived by the law that set the will of God before them. How did Christ deal with this? "And the scribes and Pharisees brought unto him a woman taken in adultery; and when they had set her in the midst, they say unto him, master, this woman was taken in adultery, in the very act. Now Moses in the law commanded us that such should be stoned: but what sayest thou?"

Jesus stooped down and wrote something into the body of the earth, the earth which is the bearer of human destiny and of which he was to say, "This is my body". He had also said, "I am come to fulfil the law", that is, to bring the law as it has been till now to a conclusion. He continued to write, "as though he heard them not". But when they importuned him further for an answer he rose and said, "He that is without sin among you, let him first cast a stone at her." He continued to write into the earth .– was it to inscribe into her history the arrival of the new law? "And they, which heard it, being convicted by their own conscience, went out one by one, beginning at the eldest . . ." Jesus looking up found the woman alone, and asked her where were her accusers, "hath no man condemned thee?" She said, no man, Lord. And Jesus said unto her, neither do I condemn thee: go, and sin no more."

It is to be noted that there is no question here of remission of sins as commonly interpreted. Each one still has to awaken his conscience to deal with his own sin, otherwise there would be no room for freedom. It is the redemption of the earth from the cosmic sin of Lucifer that Christ took upon him. And even if men atone for their own sins, each sin committed does injury to the earth, and that Christ took upon him.

And now, can one imagine a brow meeting the world with purest, pristine wonder? Can one see the middle features of a face expressive of unbounded compassion? Can one recognize in the lower part of the face, in the way the jaw is formed, the very embodiment of unswerving conscience – the upholding of the world in all righteousness?

Out of these three qualities did Rudolf Steiner set out to carve a countenance. It had to transcend anything pertaining to the fallen man for Christ was sinless. When Mary Magdalene beheld the risen one she did not recognize him. She addressed him as the gardener. In the spirit he was not as she had seen him. It was when she heard his voice that she knew him.

With these qualities of wonder, compassion and conscience Rudolf Steiner connects the mission of the earth. The *opportunity* has been given by the earth to acquire them and in doing so to become truly man. The countenance, as Rudolf Steiner finally conceived it, transcends the earthly human for the divinely human – a countenance in which nevertheless every human countenance has some part.

The work however went much further resulting in a carving in wood some thirty feet high, a focal point for the great Goetheanum building then being erected. We can only single out some of the main features to give a bare indication of what was here attempted.

Commanding the whole and occupying a central place is a figure, more than full-size, upright yet no way static, with the right foot as though stepping forward. In the whole carving Lucifer and Ahriman are twice represented in totally different situations. To the right of the central figure (to the onlooker's left) Lucifer and Ahriman are as though suspended: they appear at first sight as though locked closely together. Lucifer hovers above, with wing-like structures billowing over his head, his lower figure dwindling almost to a tail the end of which curls upward. Below, Ahriman, his bony wings closely contracted to the sides, with claw-like hands, reaches up as though to grip the suspended curled-up tail of Lucifer. At a casual glance they might seem to be intimately united, yet, in fact, they are in bitterest strife. Lucifer, with his bird-like upward lifting gesture, would seem to scorn the world below, his one intention being to wrest the soul of man away from the

The Group. Foto-Gmelin.

earth and carry it off to a kingdom of his own. Ahriman, on the contrary, wishes to hornify or mineralize the body of man and make it earth-bound for ever. Thus the two figures are in a state of arrested strife for the possession of the one object, man, yet there is no space left for him between them. Their apparent interlocking thus covers their desperate strife. To their left, more greatly proportioned, with forward glance, is the central figure, called by Rudolf Steiner *The Representative of Man*. This figure has his left arm upraised with an inclination leftwards, where we see Lucifer tumbling headlong downwards as from a height above – having, as Rudolf Steiner describes it, broken his own wings in unspeakable agony at beholding 'the true light that lighteth every man'.

The right arm of that central figure is pointing strongly downwards with an inclination to the right (to our left as we face him) where, sunk below the earth, his wings contracted, his sharp features defiantly looking upwards, we see Ahriman, thrust down as though overwhelmed by the moral force in all its pristine strength which he is obliged to suffer.

There is no trace of tension, of attack or defence, in the central figure, only his presence, in every detail the god of balance between the other two, from above and below, from right to left, even from behind forward as expressed in the advancing right foot, and the countenance in its threefoldness expressive of the three qualities described previously.

High up on our left, above the interlocked figures, and peeping down as though from behind a parapet, is a third figure observing the drama taking place below, not directly engaged, or not yet.

As we face this carving we are reminded how each one, in the fulfilment of his destiny, must inevitably find himself, not once but many times, somewhere between Lucifer and Ahriman. Awakened to the right quality of wonder he may expel the false light of Lucifer, possessed with a right conscience for truth he may quell the unrightful powers of Ahriman, filled with heart's compassion for the world, he may learn to know his brotherhood in Christ. Nothing imposes on the onlooker. Only the example stands before him. But he may also know that human destiny is a stage upon which higher destinies unfold. In this age of freedom, human destiny is raised to a new level, for insofar as man becomes a conscious participator in the shaping of the future, acting out of the freedom of his own spirit, he begins to take a new rôle in the world process. Through the Christ he is raised to the level of being the youngest hierarchy in the order of creation. Christ said of John the Baptist who ushered in the new age, "he was the greatest born of woman, yet less than the angels". And man, today, finding himself at the heralding of a new age of light, is called on to awaken in himself that which carries beyond nature to a birth in the spirit. Man, so far less than the angels, may yet regard himself cosmically as their younger brother. That great carving speaks for the very heart of anthroposophy.

We may well ask what is the destiny of such beings as Lucifer and Ahriman. That is equivalent to asking what is the origin of evil and must it be perpetuated. Such questions lead far beyond the scope of this small book, yet there are one or two observations we might make.

Such beings as Lucifer and Ahriman, as we confront them, appear to have lost all initiatives in regard to themselves. They work as nature forces impervious to appeal. They are obliged to be as they are and to act as they do, always in opposition to the beneficent powers who have the guidance of human destiny.

It is through the deed of Lucifer that humanity has sunk more deeply into matter than would otherwise have been the case, and has thereby also fallen a prey to Ahriman. The direct effect is this separation through the densified body from the surrounding world. But this is the very pre-condition, as we have seen, for developing the qualities whereby, through the deed of Christ, man can awaken to his own identity upon the path to freedom. In a sense we are indebted to these adverse powers though they on their own part can only act to destroy man.

Whereas the good powers hold back, as we have seen, in the case of Michael, and Christ himself, to make room for man to realize and advance in freedom, these other powers are ever insinuating themselves to rob him of his freedom. Rudolf Steiner in his mystery plays gives much evidence of this and how, in the course of development, they have to be met, and above all recognized for what they are.

At the same time, held within the right bounds, they have great gifts for man. Lucifer with his upward-lifting nature inspires the impulse to art, to lift life above the common-place, but if unchecked it leads to egotism and extrava-gance. Ahriman is the genius behind technical invention. The human being acquires great conscientiousness and responsibility in handling the physical: these qualities if not then turned to inner work, lead man to the illusion that the world is nothing but a machine and he a cog in it.

We have to realize that these powers are not only outside us; they are in us and a part of our nature; they are in our blood and nerve. We cannot escape them, we can only transform them so that through man, in the far distant future, they may gain some measure of redemption. For example, we little realize the power of our self-love. We can cure ourselves of Lucifer by directing that love away from ourselves and into the world – we can practise increasing our love for the world. We also are coldly indifferent to the things of the world under the mask of objectivity. We can practise turning this objectivity back on ourselves, make use of Ahriman to grow more objective to ourselves.

In this way a more conscious attitude can enter our daily lives beneficially. We are brought back to the early section of this book dealing with exercises. Even such great considerations can be brought into immediate service.

Yet the adversaries still remain adversaries and will do so for long ages to come taking a new form with man's every step in progress. At this time, at the passage from Kali-yuga into a new age of light, we are heavily beset within and without. It is not only that we confront such perils as are released in atomic energy. The growing bewilderment and increasing helplessness in the world serve as preparation for what has long been foreseen as the advent of a stage of world dictatorship for the extermination of every form of inner freedom, and the creation of every form of unfreedom. Ahriman will provide the machine under the pretence of orderly living and Lucifer will provide every form of licence in the name of freedom. This century has already, in a preliminary way, been a witness of this.

Tragedy and comedy lie deep at the roots of human life and culture. Tragedy is separation, falling apart, becoming lost to one another. Comedy is uniting, meeting again, finding one another. In the great mystery of life every separation overcome leads to a greater meeting. Separation is the price for freedom. Love is the only uniting force. The great gift that mankind is destined to bring into the universe is that of love born of freedom – love in freedom.

If the Anti-Christ should come, as in the light of anthroposophy appears to be inevitable and very near our time, the Christ himself is surely there to reveal himself anew to the souls of men. The Anti-Christ we must learn to recognize, for that defeats him. Christ waits to be received. Our age requires the birth of a heightened consciousness through self-endeavour – a new degree of selflessness and service. The way is open. It rests only with the human will.

Who is the Anti-Christ? This question touches on the deepest secrets of our time. We can only give an indication for further thought and study.

We have entered the age of post-Kaliyuga, an age of the

dawning of a new spiritual consciousness in man, an age whose sustaining strength will be the progressive awakening of mankind to the risen Christ where he dwells in the etheric world, a world of light and life immediately adjoining the earth. It may also be called the age of the second coming which Christ Himself foretold as described in the Gospels of Saint Matthew, Mark and Luke. He gives warning of false Christs and prophets who will show "signs and wonders to seduce, if it were possible, even the elect". He points to a time of great tribulation, fathers against sons and sons against fathers, nation rising against nation and kingdom against kingdom, earthquakes, famines, pestilences, "these are the beginning of sorrows." There will also be signs in the heavens, in sun, and moon, and stars. "And then shall they see the son of man coming in the clouds with great power and glory."

Rudolf Steiner in 1909 and 1910 and also later declared that the age of the second advent has indeed begun, that from the 1930s on, first a very few, and then gradually more will behold 'Christ in the clouds', or, in anthroposophical language, 'Christ in the etheric' in ways akin to Paul's experience at Damascus, and this will continue until, in the space of two thousand five hundred years the whole of humanity will have reached that experience.

It would follow then that the adversaries of whom Christ spoke whose aim it must be to obscure totally the vision and the understanding for the Risen One will gather up all their opposing strength at this time.

Rudolf Steiner reveals that Lucifer walked the earth in a human body in the third millennium BC. It follows inevitably, therefore, in the course of history, that Ahriman will similarly be incarnated in the third millennium AD. We would expect him to present himself as a great benefactor, bringing peace and plenty to all but in such a way that every vestige of human freedom will be obliterated. His vast but freezing cold intelligence can only serve as ideal, the absolute impeccability of the perfect machine. The world is to be his machine, and humanity emptied of heart and soul its crowning piece. We may recognize how much preparation to that end is already in vogue.

We are in an epoch with Christ in the etheric waiting for man to awaken to the full meaning of his words "I am with you always" and Ahriman who is to appear in outer form on earth as Anti-Christ to pursue further his work of plunging mankind into uttermost darkness.

When we think of Lucifer incarnated in the ancient east, of Christ in the three years as Jesus of Nazareth from the baptism by Jordan to the death on the cross, and Ahriman approaching incarnation in the modern west, and see in this a drama of the gods around the being of man we encounter once again the profound significance of the great carving with Christ between Lucifer and Ahriman, and we may ask why Rudolf Steiner chose to describe that central figure as *The Representative of Man.*

Postscript

THE GREAT CARVING, often referred to as the Group, has a noble space allotted to it high up in the Goetheanum at Dornach, near Basle. It was originally intended for a very different place. Where the Goetheanum now stands, on that same foundation, there once stood another Goetheanum, a totally different building, two-domed, all of wood, a unique structure that had not its like on earth. Rudolf Steiner had designed it in every detail. Many new impulses of art had gone into its inner and outer formation. Ten years of continuous labour went into it. It was spoken of as the House of the Word. Then, in the course of one night, December 31st, 1922, it was completely burned down by an act of arson similar to that which burnt down the Temple of Ephesus. Whereas that Temple, also dedicated to the Mystery of the Word, was the crowning and last great school of the Greek mysteries, the first Goetheanum had been conceived to bear witness to the new mysteries of the present time. The Group was not yet completed and therefore was not in the building, and so, by great good fortune, has been preserved for us.

The destruction of that building, after so much love and devotion had gone into it on the part of many, was a great blow. For Rudolf Steiner, the greatest sorrow was that western eyes in particular would never be able to behold its life-kindling forms.

A year later, during the Christmas week of 1923 leading into New Year's Day, 1924, Rudolf Steiner refounded the Society and gave it a new form. It was to be called the

The First Goetheanum.

The Second Goetheanum.

General Anthroposophical Society and all national societies were to be part of it. The Society was to be open unconditionally to all who had an interest in anthroposophy and its further progress. It was in every sense a 'free' society. In addition, Rudolf Steiner called into being a School of Spiritual Science or High School for furthering the work of anthroposophy. In connection with it he established a number of sections to carry particular studies to greater depth and to encourage research.

As a matter of historic interest we list the Sections as they were first founded, and the appointed leaders at the time.

The fine arts and literature	Albert Steffen
The performing arts,	
Speech, Drama, Eurythmy	Marie Steiner
Medicine	Ita Wegman
Astronomy and Mathematics	Elizabeth Vreede
Science	Guenther Wachsmuth
Education	Rudolf Steiner in union
	with the other section leaders

The above named are no longer living but the work represented by the Sections has spread far through the world.

The present Goetheanum was also designed by Rudolf Steiner. He wrote:

For a year I carried about with me the idea for a new Goetheanum. The transformation of this idea out of wood, into the artistically brittle substance of concrete was not easy. Then, at the beginning of this year, I began to work on the formation of the model . . . For many years, in my anthroposophical writings and lectures, I have emphasized the fact that anthroposophy is not only a theoretical conception of the world, but that a special style in art results from its very nature. And, since that is the case, a building for anthroposophy must grow out of this itself . . .

By the very fact that the second Goetheanum is so very different from the first, we can learn that in spiritual life nothing can be merely repeated. Each fresh endeavour calls for a new deed of creation. This second Goetheanum has inspired many to see how forms in space, entering the eye, can quicken an awakening life experience in the beholder.

The burning of the first Goetheanum had, from all accounts, deprived Rudolf Steiner of much strength. In the period following the establishment of the General Anthroposophical Society, his physical strength was depleted still further, yet never had he worked so hard as in the months that followed.

Marie Steiner, his wife, writes of him in connection with this period:

> Every day, three courses manifesting an inexpressible power of ascent of the spirit. In addition at least three lectures every week about anthroposophy and magnificent lectures for those working on the building. One dared not utter a word about sparing him. Pleas to spare himself constituted a hindrance.

In addition, "The door-keepers counted four hundred visitors during the time when he was daily giving four lectures."

In June 1924, he inaugurated at the request of farmers a new way of agriculture now widely known and practised as Biodynamic Agriculture.

In August 1924, he made his last visit to England, and amongst much else gave a lecture course on education directed towards the founding (which took place) of the first English speaking Waldorf School based on the Waldorf School in Stuttgart which he himself had founded in 1919.

On 28th September 1924, the eve of Michaelmas, he gave his last lecture. He did not appear in public again.

Dr Wachsmuth, who was his daily attendant and messenger at this time, writes: "Lying in his room, he loved the living noise of hammering and scaffold-building which penetrated from the building place of the Goetheanum into the quiet of his sick room, announcing the building in the process of coming into being." But he did not live to see it.

Each week he sent in a hand-written article for members dealing with one aspect or another of Michael's battle for man, now with Lucifer, now with Ahriman, and always in intimate connection with the Christ – a marvellous concentration of material for study and for meditative work.

But, according to Dr Wachsmuth who had to supply him with these things, "he also did a tremendous amount of reading, keeping himself continuously informed regarding literature newly published in the fields of science, art, history, and all others."

He died on the thirtieth day of March, 1925.

Dr Wachsmuth: "The forward-striding figure of the Christ statue, pointing into the expanses of the universe, which he himself had created and at whose feet he now lay, spoke for the eye of those left behind on the earth what was here taking place for the spirit of a great human being, who had dedicated his life to the annunciation of the Christ."

The work he initiated in so many fields has continued to grow and expand and has reached all lands where a free spiritual and cultural life is possible.

The unfolding of Rudolf Steiner's anthroposophical work covers a relatively short period of time, 1902-1925. It ranges from great cosmic conceptions to a deep engagement in the arts, leading on to a detailed consideration of some of the practical fields of work. At the end, beholding the human being in the light of all this, one could well say, *Lo, this is man!*

The cosmic aspect not only includes descriptions of the

hierarchical beings directly concerned with human and world evolution, but also offers a basis for the study of the heavenly bodies, stars, sun, moon, and planets in their present influences on nature and on man. This has proved greatly enlightening to the practising teacher, doctor and farmer.

What came strongly to expression in the arts was the principle of metamorphosis, of organic progress and transformation. This was clearly to be seen in the architecture, the sculpture and the painting of the first Goetheanum. All these three arts received new impulses whereby what is an underlying creative principle in nature is raised to new modes of realization through man. The mystery plays made similar demands for a new art of theatre in regard to mode of speech, dramatic gesture, music, colour and form. Speech formation (*Sprach-gestaltung*) was developed into an art in itself.

Here special mention may be made of Eurythmy, a new art of movement initiated by Rudolf Steiner, described also as visible speech and visible song. It is an art in which motion and gesture have their origin in the primordial sources of the elements of language and of music out of which the human form has been engendered. Therefore it can translate itself with equal immediacy into every language and given mode of music. In this art, light and colour also play a great part.

In the last years, from 1917 on, anthroposophy reached quite specially into the practical spheres of daily life; into medicine, including cancer research, and the production of a new range of medicaments, mainly homeopathic, for internal and external treatment; into a new art of education, more generally known as Waldorf education, and, as a parallel but independent development, curative education; into a new science of agriculture, (biodynamics) which extends the work to engage the instreaming light forces from the starry and planetary spaces; into research in mathematics and in various scientific fields.

In addition to all else, in response to a request from a number of pastors he conducted special studies with them and later enabled them on their responsibility to found the Church of the Christian Community in 1922 for the renewal of religious life out of a renewed understanding of the sacraments. The new Church was under the leadership of Dr Friedrich Rittelmeyer.

All this activity was released within the first quarter of this century, toward the emergence, out of our materialistic times, of a new era of culture, well schooled in the disciplines of scientific method and observation, but directed to include the supersensible realities of human existence. This is the deeper lying meaning of the word anthroposophy, with its implication, *a way of life*.

Bibliography

BOOKS BY RUDOLF STEINER MENTIONED IN THIS BOOK

Goethe's World Conception
The Philosophy of Freedom
Christianity as Mystical Fact
Knowledge of Higher Worlds
Theosophy
Occult Science – an Outline
Cosmic Memory (Atlantis and Lemuria)
Lectures on the Gospels: St John
Lectures on the Gospels: St Luke
Lectures on the Gospels: St Matthew
Lectures on the Gospels: St Mark
The Threefold Social Order
The Portal of Initiation (in: Four Mystery Dramas)
The Course of my Life

RECOMMENDED BOOKS BY OTHER AUTHORS

A. C. Harwood: *The Way of a Child*
   The Recovery of Man in Childhood
Francis Edmunds: *Rudolf Steiner Education – the Waldorf*
   Schools
   Anthroposophy as a Healing Force
Owen Barfield: *Romanticism comes of Age*
   Saving the Appearances
Hermann Poppelbaum: *Man and Animal*
Ernst Lehrs: *Man or Matter*
Walther Bühler: *Living with your Body*
Theodor Schwenk: *Sensitive Chaos*
George Adams & Olive Whicher: *The Plant between Sun and*
   Earth
Friederich Rittelmeyer: *Rudolf Steiner enters my Life*
Johannes Hemleben: *Rudolf Steiner*
A. P. Shepherd: *A Scientist of the Invisible*
Emil Bock: *The Three Years (The Life of Christ between*
   Baptism and Ascension)
Stewart Easton: *Man and World in the Light of*
   Anthroposophy
   Rudolf Steiner, Herald of a New Epoch
Herbert Koepf, B. D. Pettersen & W. Schaumann:
   Biodynamic Agriculture – an Introduction